SO-AKG-815

PRAISE FOR
Tim Eisenhauer and
Who the Hell Wants to Work for You?

"Absolutely fantastic, easy to read, and loaded with information you can use to transform your workplace."
— ALAN COLLINS, best-selling author and former VP of HR at PepsiCo

"Read a few chapters and—I promise—you won't be able to put it down. It's a page turner."
— JOHN JIANG, Head of HR, Lloyd's Register, Greater China

"The world needs this book! Tim's insights turn employee engagement on its head, his stories are very engaging, and it's an addicting read."
— JESSICA MEHRING, CEO of Horizon Peak Consulting and creator of The Content Lab

"I never expected it to be such good reading. I couldn't stop once I started. It's a treasure chest of inspiration for our company. And it's worth every single penny of your investment. Highly recommended."
— KAREN L. MORKHOLT, HR Manager and Legal Adviser

"Tim's strategies are backed up by a ton of research, case studies, and hilarious personal stories. His ideas have a huge positive impact not just on employee engagement, but on the overall performance at work."
— FARA JAZA, HR Director

"*Who the Hell Wants to Work for You?* is a new way of solving an old problem: how to get your employees to bring their A-game to work. It's all in here, from self-help to management techniques, to things you forgot and things you need to implement today."
— SAMMY TOVAR, Former Domestic Operations Manager, Mail Boxes Etc. and licensed expert Realtor

"Tim tears apart everything you knew about employee engagement and breaks it down to the basics. Do what he says and you'll build a high performing workplace you can be proud of. Highly recommended."
— CHUCK VIGEANT, President and CEO, Clearify, Inc.

"This is a book that I suggest all managers, executives, and aspiring leaders read. It's packed with case studies of what to do and what not to do, tied together with personal stories that bring the topic of employee engagement to a level everyone can understand."
— JOHN FIKE, President, WheatgrassLove

MASTERING EMPLOYEE ENGAGEMENT

WHO
THE HELL
WANTS TO WORK
FOR YOU

TIM EISENHAUER

RESULTRIS PUBLISHING

Published in the United States by Resultris Publishing.
10251 Vista Sorrento Parkway, Suite 280, San Diego, CA 92121, USA

Copyright © 2018 by Tim Eisenhauer

In accordance with the U.S. Copyright Act of 1976, the scanning, uploading, and electronic sharing of any part of this book without the permission of the publisher constitute unlawful piracy and theft of the author's intellectual property. If you would like to use material from the book (other than for review purposes), prior written permission must be obtained by contacting the publisher at permissions@resultris.com. Thank you for your support of the author's rights. Purchase only authorized editions.

Eisenhauer, Tim
Who the Hell Wants to Work for You? Mastering Employee Engagement. / Tim Eisenhauer

Includes bibliographical references.
ISBN: 978-0-9977989-0-6 (hardcover)
ISBN: 978-0-9977989-1-3 (paperback)
ISBN: 978-0-9977989-2-0 (ebook)

Version_1

To Mom and Dad.
One step closer to the island.

CONTENTS

WHEN YOU GET TO THE BOTTOM OF IT

How well you do as an employee depends on how badly you want to do the work you are doing.

How well you do as a manager depends on how many people want to work for you.

And how well you do as a company depends on how much everyone wants to work towards a common goal.

That's the essence of *employee engagement* that stumps so many people these days. Of course, most people are not stumped about what employee engagement is. They are stumped because they don't know how to make people want something they don't seem to want.

As a manager, you want your people to own their tasks, learn from their mistakes, and work well together. When this doesn't happen, your instincts tell you that people are the problem. And that you need to force, trick, or bribe them into mending their ways.

Your instincts aren't wrong. Whatever you choose to believe, you will find plenty of evidence to support your view. Your outcomes will faithfully match your attitude. Which is why we will be paying close attention throughout this book to how you think about your employees.

What if you assumed that people naturally love to work? That they long to contribute? And that they are only truly happy when working together towards something they see as bigger than themselves?

If you look at it this way, there is nothing to fix. People are already wired to work with passion if … their work environment calls for it. Who is responsible for your employees' work environment? That's right, you are.

I wrote *Who the Hell Wants to Work for You?* to help managers and business owners, myself included, eliminate the root causes of conflict and controversy in the workplace. There are hacks and tricks in here as well, but they are not important in themselves. Once you focus on the essentials, you will be able to come up with your own strategies, as did the companies whose stories you'll see here.

This book contains twenty-three workplace principles. The principles express the most common needs of people at work. I am convinced that every company that wants to be successful in the long run must meet these needs or pay the price.

The principles work universally. The obvious, the not-so-obvious—and the I-don't-care-what-Facebook-does-we-are-not-them. The best way to benefit from the book is *to assume that they apply in your case.*

In Part One, *Empower the Individual,* we'll talk about selecting, training, and motivating people to do their best work.

In Part Two, *Empower the Relationship,* we will look at the part the manager plays in engaging his team.

Part Three, *Empower the Culture,* is about executive leadership and its power to create and sustain an engaged workforce.

If one of these principles looks like a standard practice already, ask in what ways you may yet fall short. For the pies-in-the-sky and cans-of-worms, ask yourself, what about the principle you find appealing and how you could make it work for you. We will be looking at lots of examples, so you'll see what each principle means to different employers—and what it doesn't need to mean. In the end, you may decide that certain stones are better left unturned, at least for the time being. But you will never view people management through the same set of eyes.

Tim Eisenhauer

THE DAWN OF A NEW ERA

> ❝ We start from the presumption that our people are talented and want to contribute. We accept that, without meaning to, our company is stifling that talent in myriad unseen ways. Finally, we try to identify those impediments and fix them. ❞
>
> — ED CATMULL, Co-founder and CEO of Pixar, *Creativity, Inc.*

THE PAST

Hating your job used to be the norm.

As recently as 2004, author-blogger D. JoAnne Swanson gave this heartfelt definition of the word *job*:

> *JOB: Drudgery. Alienated effort expended for someone else on their terms, often a corporation or boss, doing something you don't care about, in exchange for external compensation—money, health insurance, benefits, pleasing others. Something done against one's will for the sake of a paycheck.*[1]

Back when I was in college, few of us looked to jobs for personal fulfillment. It never even occurred to us. If you wanted self-expression, you started a garage band. If you wanted to serve your fellow man, you joined the Peace Corps. Paid work was reserved for activities you would not otherwise perform—the more objectionable the job, the higher the paycheck. Crowning the list were the "real jobs" you got upon graduation.

We had excellent reasons to be weary of grown-up jobs. Far from allaying our worst fears, most companies worked hard to reinforce them. From day one. Like this character from Jordan Belfort's *The Wolf of Wall Street*:

> "… *Your job"—he looked at the plastic nametag on my cheap blue lapel—"Jordan Belfort, is a connector, which means you'll be dialing the phone five hundred times a day, trying to get past the secretaries. You're not trying to sell anything or recommend anything or create anything. You are just trying to get a business owner on the phone." He paused for a brief instant, then spewed out more venom. "And when you do get one on the phone, all you'll say is: Hello, Mr. So and So, I have Scott holding for you, and then you pass the phone to me and start dialing again. Think you can handle that, or is it too complicated for you?"* (Jordan Belfort, *The Wolf of Wall Street*)[2]

I resisted getting a real job for as long as I could. Finally, in the summer between my fifth and sixth year of college, I caved in to pressure from a girl I was dating and typed up my first résumé. It was a take-no-prisoners attempt at making white space look appealing. Extra-wide margins. My name in big letters. And the telltale word "RESUME" across the top.

The girl had an aunt who worked for the local chain of beauty salons and schools and knew someone in the corporate IT. The résumé wound up in the hands of the IT director who, as luck would have it, used to referee my high school basketball games. I was invited for an interview and, after forty-five minutes of reminiscing about my athletic past, I had a $10-an-hour internship at the IT help desk.

The year was 2001. Apple was about to release its first iPod. Grain traders in Sub-Saharan Africa started using cell phones to check crop prices. Jimmy Wales and Larry Sanger launched Wikipedia. And thirty-year-old Elon Musk set his sights on PayPal. Yet surfing the tidal waves of digital revolution was a low priority for the beauty conglomerate.

Instead, my new employer used my raw talent to (a) replace keyboards after countless employees spilled coffee on them (they were all shocked when I told them that the little pop-out tray with a hole in the middle was a CD ROM drive, and not an ergonomically designed coffee-cup holder); (b) wipe porn off hard drives; and (c) deal with a variety of complaints, all of which led back to human hair trapped in hard-to-reach parts of the computer.

The overabundance of hair in the office equipment was a mystery to me—that is, until I was on my third office job and my own hair started falling out from stress and depression. But that was later. The truth was, I didn't mind my internship, boring and disgusting as it was.

You see, Beauty Co. wasn't my first real-world job. Two years earlier, I had dropped out of college to become an electrician. Then, a year into my apprenticeship, I suddenly rediscovered the joy of higher learning. It happened at the exact moment when my foreman told me to plunge into a six-foot-deep mud hole and pull wires. I promptly returned to school and immersed myself into programming and IT management.

Have you ever wondered why people hate their jobs, but don't quit them? My story taught me that it's not so much for lack of a better alternative, as it is for fear of a more miserable one. No matter how passionately you hate your own job, you are equally grateful for not having to do someone else's. And so, you cling to the precious few perks your job affords. Add in fixed expenses, like rent and student loans, and you begin to see why the majority of my generation chose to suffer in silence.

THE PRESENT

And yet better days were coming. While I was working the IT help desk under the micromanaging eye of my boss, a stockbroker by the name of Jordan Belfort had already made and lost a fortune in Stratton Oakmont.

Belfort was convicted of defrauding thousands of clients. The National Association of Securities Dealers shut down his firm. But that's not why he is enjoying a second career as a motivational speaker and best-selling author.

One former employee described Stratton Oakmont as *"the craziest place I ever worked at and the most exciting given the very real prospect of making millions of dollars."* The most unusual part about Belfort's infamous brainchild is that it was a place where people loved to come to work.

Its rogue ways notwithstanding, Stratton actually obeyed the laws of employee engagement to a tee: (a) authentic values—in Stratton's case, unabashed greed and drunken delirium; (b) unique culture—strippers, drugs, prostitutes, and public humiliation of brokers who didn't drive luxury sports cars; (c) transparency—about pushing worthless securities onto gullible customers; (d) camaraderie—throwing mega parties to bring employees together; (e) frequent and spontaneous dialogue—completely uncensored; and (f) wealth sharing—empowering people to make millions overnight.

The result was a fantastically, if briefly, successful company.

Today, employee-friendly practices are the stuff of which *Fortune's* "100 Best Companies to Work For" are made. Some of them, like Zappo's Bald and Blue days (a company tradition where employees bond over buzz cuts), may look like a scene from the movie *The Wolf of Wall Street*. While others, like corporate volunteering, are worlds apart.

Not every successful company is a model of employee engagement. But those that do take care of employees in the right way are ahead of the game. In the coming chapters we will take a detailed look at both these companies' methods and their results. I took many of my examples from *Fortune's* 2014 list. I also snooped around Glassdoor and Quora to see what people were saying about their award-winning employers after-hours.

THE FUTURE

Do you know that, in many important ways, you can tell the future? That's because the future doesn't arrive to all of us at the same time. Like sunrise, it makes several stops in remote locations before it reaches your door. My point here is that, while your company may be wholly or partially entrenched in the past, someone at this very moment is living the future.

Your future.

That's all good in hindsight, you say. But from where I'm sitting, how do I know that someone's wacky way of expressing corporate identity is the missing link to my company's future?

Don't worry, it isn't. This book is about people-management practices that are common to all companies who "get" employees—even though some of these practices may be a stretch, at best, for the rest of the world. For now. Researchers, consultants, famous CEOs, and people who plain and simple know how to work with other people, all agree that these are the ways of the future.

Look, I came all the way from life-imitating *Office Space,* to a company I love to work for. And I can tell you that I am never going back. That's how I know the future is already here. People just like you and me are making the same journey as we speak. They are leaving jobs, bosses and companies that make them sick and finding ones that make them happy. This is a trend you can count on. And, like any trend, you can use it to your advantage.

PART ONE
EMPOWER THE INDIVIDUAL

❝You have to enable and empower people to make decisions independent of you. As I've learned, each person on a team is an extension of your leadership; if they feel empowered by you they will magnify your power to lead.**❞**

— TOM RIDGE, Governor of Pennsylvania 1995–2001

❝I want to empower women. I want people to be afraid of the women I dress.**❞**

— ALEXANDER MCQUEEN

❝I'm thrilled to continue my partnership with U by Kotex for Generation Know while helping to empower girls.**❞**

— KHLOE KARDASHIAN

CHAPTER 1
AN EMPLOYEE'S VIEW:
THE CUBICLE-SIDE DILEMMA

❝ I'm a big fan of relaxing and not having a schedule. That's my best way to keep from going crazy. ❞
— OLIVIA THIRLBY, Actress

❝ The entire economic system depends on the fact that people are willing to do unpleasant things in return for money. ❞
— SCOTT ADAMS, *The Joy of Work*

"Who are these employee-friendly companies?"

Betsy's question was no idle curiosity. She was about to quit a well-paying and interesting job for which she was amply qualified. Reason: extreme difficulty in accomplishing anything. Result: frustration, anxiety, self-doubt, apathy and stress. Betsy decided enough was enough.

Betsy's company hired her to launch an ambitious new line of services. The board enthusiastically approved her strategy. However, at the execution stage, the project ran into massive resistance. Too many decision-makers. Meaning lots of people who could tentatively say no, and no one to authoritatively say yes. In the finest tradition of corporate red tape, "no" didn't come as a one-syllable word. It came as endless, meaningless, and conflicting requests for changes and clarifications.

Betsy put in three years' worth of valiant effort. After that, she learned to bide her time in the office by answering questions and requests with questions and requests—while job searching like crazy to get herself the hell outta there.

In the language of business psychologists, Betsy *disengaged*. That is, she quit mentally or lost interest before she actually quit her job. Business psychologists have a name for Betsy's condition because they have stumbled upon an intriguing link between engagement and performance. Believe it or not, how well a business does is directly proportionate to how many employees give a hot damn about their work.

The importance of keeping people motivated took the business world by storm. It's not that they hadn't thought of it before. They just didn't realize to what extent motivation was lacking in the workplace. I am going to excuse myself from quoting exact numbers. They will be obsolete by the time you read this book, anyway. Plus, your industry and company might be better or worse off than the average. But if you subscribe to any business periodicals, like *The Wall Street Journal* or *Forbes*—or if you read stuff online—you already know that the stats are dismal. A vast majority of U.S. employees hate their jobs. The odds are high that some of these people work for you, more so if yours is a large company.

Gloomy headlines in business periodicals are not, by themselves, a cause for concern. There's always someone somewhere crying wolf. On a close examination, they usually turn out to be vendors and consultants eager to sell you wolf-hunting weapons. Or, at the very least, a fat report on how many wolves have been spotted in your neighborhood. Journalists get all over bad news, too. Apparently, it makes better news, and they, too, can sell more of it faster.

Once upon a time I had faith in so-called independent researchers. That was until a well-known firm approached me to "win an industry award" in exchange for an amount of money so obscene that I wasn't even tempted. After "painstakingly evaluating" several of my competitors, they found what they were looking for: another endorsement-starved seller. The company is now proudly displaying the "award" on its website, as if they had actually won it!

That said, have no doubt: there's never been a better time to ask yourself if people really want to work for you and the company you represent. The cult following of the 1999 movie *Office Space* was an early indication. Another one is the fact that the *Dilbert* comic strip has become a staple in PowerPoint slides around the world. Apparently, these days cynical office humor never falls on deaf ears.

Here's Scott Adams, the creator of *Dilbert,* explaining the rise of cubicle-side discontent:

> *Two hundred years ago, for example, a few extra dollars meant the difference between sleeping cozily indoors versus shivering under a pile of leaves until you were eaten by coyotes. ... Money is no longer the difference between life and death for most white collar workers. If you have a reasonable job, money can't buy nearly as much happiness as it used to.*
> (Scott Adams, *The Joy of Work*)

In other words, people no longer work just to survive. For the most part, they take life for granted, and they want more out of it than a pleasant driving experience to and from the office. In fact, our brains require all kinds of stimulation. We crave things like: autonomy: directing our own lives; mastery: getting better at something that matters to us; purpose: making a difference; success: making progress towards goals; and community: social interaction.

The first three are from Daniel H. Pink's book *Drive: The Surprising Truth About What Motivates Us*. Pink argues that people want these things more than they want money and stuff—an idea you may or may not find surprising. However, here's the real paradox. Doesn't it often seem like people (a) hate thinking for themselves; (b) are perfectly happy and even proud to be clueless; and (c) given a choice between making a difference and watching funny cat videos, overwhelmingly choose the latter?

Who is right? Is Pink talking about *real* employees? Your employees? Or hypothetical ideal employees who pose for the company brochure and quit before anyone has had a chance to observe them firsthand?

The surprising truth is that you won't know until you've given your employees a full shot at autonomy, mastery, and purpose. People won't change your opinion of them, unless you treat them better than what you think they deserve. So, no matter how incapable you believe your employees to be, go ahead and give them another chance to prove you wrong!

I added the last two items, *success* and *community,* because they seemed like no-brainers. Who doesn't want to look good (success) in front of other people (community)? And even when there's no one to applaud your accomplishments, there is always that voice in your head that loves pointing out what a loser you are. You want to look good in front of it, too.

Our productive brain is like a computer screen: if you don't touch the keypad, it goes to sleep. We may look like we are working, but we are not really focused on the task at hand. The emotional pull that helps us find the right solution at the right time is gone. We are just running the clock and collecting paychecks. Engagement drivers, like the five above, are the keys. Touch any one of them, and the light comes on. The computer *and the person* are no longer simply occupying a desk; they are *on*.

The drivers are always present. When our job feeds them, we feel empowered:

- We own projects and tasks
- We are clear about goals and expectations
- We act decisively on the company's behalf

That's the definition of an engaged employee. And, if we are well matched to the job and connected to others on the team, the results can be nothing short of spectacular.

However, when the job interferes with our genuine needs, we fight-or-flight and our work suffers. Take Betsy's case, for example. She had to jump through hoops to move the project along—loss of autonomy. She was asked to perform meaningless tasks—loss of purpose. As a result, she wasn't able to deliver on her objectives—loss of success.

On the plus side, Betsy's job had lots of visibility and interaction. The people around Betsy kept her interested, even if they didn't fully empower her—community. The lack of support was an opportunity for Betsy to become a stronger leader—mastery. Those were the things that kept her going for as long as she did.

To be fair, being empowered is a state of mind. You cannot disempower anyone without his or her consent. The problem starts when companies place too much of a burden on the employees for empowering themselves. Wanted ads are full of demand for result-oriented self-starters, as though these were immutable genetic traits, like eye color and fingerprints.

They are not. Psychologists are now saying that our work environment has an effect on our attitude and behavior, just as we have an effect on it. When the company itself is not wired for empowering people, self-empowered personalities are not the answer. As the following story demonstrates.

At the end of the summer, my internship with Beauty Co. turned into a regular part-time job. As I was making my keyboard-swiping, porn-wiping, hair-pulling office rounds, I heard a lot of gripes from my coworkers. It occurred to me that their struggles were not entirely self-inflicted.

The company had been on an acquisition spree. Yet the employee directory had not been updated for years. You could easily get lost in the phone system trying to locate the right person. User handbooks and company guidelines? Forget it. Most people didn't even know how to submit a problem to the help desk. Bottom line: people had no easy access to the information they needed to do their jobs.

Not only did I put my finger on an insidious threat to productivity, I also found a solution. What the company needed was an intranet—a central location where documents could be posted electronically and updated as often as necessary. Being a help-desk technician, I was eager to help. Except that building an intranet wasn't part of my job. I didn't even know how to do it. But, since I was a result-oriented self-starter, I learned what an intranet looked like and programmed one by trial and error, all on my own time.

To give you an idea of just how result-oriented I was, I took printouts of all kinds of documents that people used and typed them in by hand. I ended up retyping the entire employee handbook, working from home, between dinnertime and late-night horror movies. My alarm would go off at 6:00 in the morning. I'd get up and go to school. I'd be in the office by 11:00 a.m., clock out at 5:00, and back home to my pet project by 6:00 p.m.

In four months' time I was ready to share my creation with the world. By Beauty Co.'s low standards, it was a marvel of information technology. You could submit problems to the help desk online. You could request time off using electronic forms. (I added a calendar with the holidays for extra ease.) You could find stuff and connect with people. It even had a section for corporate news, which I fashioned out of a weekly newsletter, printed and hand-delivered to our in-baskets. What's more, it was fully user-tested—something I did during the day while fixing people's computers. I'd pull up their web browser and have them try a couple of features. They'd say, "That's cool, Tim! Can it do this other thing, too?"

When I showed it to my managers, their jaws dropped. They turned it live on the corporate network, and within weeks, hundreds of people were logging on daily. All the departments wanted in. We got swamped with requests. For a brief moment, my job didn't seem like an inspiration for weekend-long drinking binges. I could actually see myself doing it as a career. The only thing left to do was to convince my managers to hire me full-time and pay my living wage.

Back to the late-night drill. I researched and calculated cost-benefits of a robust intranet. Functional specs. Positions in the company it would eliminate. How soon it would pay for itself … I am not kidding. I really wanted that damn job! I printed out my sources and attached them to my report—over fifty pages in all. I even showed it to my college professor to bulletproof my case.

How much should my dream job pay? Professional developer salaries ranged from a respectable $50K all the way into six figures. I gave myself a modest raise that would have bumped my pay up to $40K per year. I figured if I came in under the market, it would clinch the deal, because there would be no way any reasonable person could object to my proposal.

And then they fired me.

At first, I didn't know what to make of it. I kept coming to the happy hours with my office buddies—why toss out the baby with the bathwater? Plus, I wanted to figure out why I got fired and what happened to my project. Pretty soon I had the full inside scoop.

While I was busy with the intranet, the company hired reorg consultants to look for inefficiencies. Yes, just like the movie *Office Space*. They found two big fat ones: my boss, the help-desk manager, and his boss, the IT director. The two of them had to think of something quick, and I walked right in with my fifty-page proposal. My friends said that after they fired me, they presented it to the higher-ups as evidence that they were on track and even one step ahead of the reorg. Then they hired an outside contractor to execute on my proposal, item by item. For all I know, they even used my salary sheets to beat down his price.

In hindsight, things worked out for the best for all involved. I got the better-paying job I was clamoring for. And my boss got to keep his. I looked him up on LinkedIn while I was writing this book, and he is still there. Imagine, the same job for twenty-two years! Makes me wonder what would have happened to me had they accepted my proposal.

Beauty Co. may be stuck in its old ways, but the rest of the world has changed for the better, right? My friend Betsy is skeptical. Her job search didn't turn up a hidden employee paradise. She is now an independent consultant. "Every company should empower employees," she concluded in her state-of-the-world-in-one-sentence way, "but I just don't see it happening."

Let's think about that. Even though companies don't set out to squelch employees, few are actually doing anything to empower them—and even fewer are doing it the right way. Now let's think about the exceptions.

Some companies willingly give their employees the keys to the kingdom. But why? What do they get in return? Extreme customer service? It certainly rings true for places like Whole Foods, Zappos, and Southwest Airlines. What about extreme innovation? Is employee empowerment-slash-engagement-slash-ecstasy the driving force behind the meteoric rise of the Web 2.0 champions, like Google, LinkedIn and Facebook?

Notice something else about these companies. They play and win in highly competitive markets. Profit margins at Whole Foods are at least twice as high as the industry average. Southwest grew in a shrinking market. And before Zappos, who would have ever thought that selling shoes online was a good idea? As for tech companies, the competition for talent is fierce, and yet the winners enjoy cult-like employee loyalty.

Forget the mythical outliers. What about the millions of small businesses who beat the dismal survival odds? Where do they find the resources to learn and grow?

Venture capital? Business plans??

Sometimes people think a business starts with a plan, and then you pay someone to execute on it. If you've ever started a business, you know that, in the end, your plan doesn't even matter. What matters are the people with whom you've partnered along the way. Often, the very idea of starting a business is a product of a relationship. And then that idea takes another idea, and another, and another before it can make it in the real world. You can never count on yourself to come up with all the ideas. Hell, you never know where the next life-saving idea will come from. Where I once saw my business plans backed up by millions in funding, I learned to see *people* and their unforeseen contributions as the true building blocks of a business.

To keep people and take full advantage of their talents, you must empower them. What exactly does that mean? As someone who has learned by trial and error, let me first tell you what empowerment *doesn't* mean.

JUST TALKING ABOUT IT

It's better to do nothing at all, than to make vague promises and leave it business as usual. If you are going to bring up empowerment, commit to following through. Baby steps are okay, as long as they make a real difference and lead to bigger moves.

STICKING IT TO THE CUSTOMER

Let's face it: nothing pumps your ego like poking fun at customers behind their backs. The infamous Stratton Oakmont wasn't the first, nor was it the last retailer to build screwing customers into a bonding ritual. Resist the temptation!

FORGETTING ABOUT MANAGEMENT AND COMMUNICATION

This one trips people up to the point where they don't even want to hear about giving employees more breathing room. "Empower" doesn't mean "disconnect." If you assign a project and don't check in until it's done, you are probably not going to get what you want. We will talk a lot in this book about keeping people on track. For now, let's just say that empowering employees doesn't mean retiring the management. That said, the role of the manager does shift from that of a gatekeeper and overseer towards a supporter and coach.

Empowerment is getting out of people's way, so they can sustain and grow the business. It's an attitude that manifests itself differently on every occasion. It can be as simple as giving people a surprise afternoon off after a busy stretch at work; or as complex as redeveloping the neighborhood around your business. It can be free, like giving your people a chance to shine—or not, like replacing outdated IT systems that age people on contact.

Empowerment in the workplace belongs with practices and priorities built into the business, not with individual employees who choose to empower themselves.

Both Betsy and I were such individuals. We hated wasting time, and, left to our own devices, we got things done. Betsy played by the rules. I would beg forgiveness rather than ask permission. Despite this fact, our two companies treated us the same—with similar outcomes. In both cases, the company lost a qualified and motivated employee and, in Betsy's case, an opportunity to play in an exciting new market. The only difference is that Betsy took three years to diplomatically engineer herself out of her job, whereas I got the boot just a few months after I self-started my intranet project.

When we empower ourselves, we benefit ourselves. Betsy and I didn't regret taking charge of our jobs, despite the backlash we got from our employers.

When we empower others, we benefit the business and our cause. Every company gives at least some employees the freedom to do their best. Is it possible to empower more people? Everyone in the company? What would it take? And what would be the outcome?

Let's talk about empowering people the right way. Most of the ideas in this book should not surprise you. They are things you knew all along that bear repeating. Not just because they help you when you follow them—but also because they hurt you when you don't.

CHAPTER 2

HIRE TRAITS AND BEHAVIORS

❝ Most managers are exceedingly bad at making hiring decisions. If you gave Charles Manson a shave and combed his bangs over the swastika on his forehead, he could get hired as the CEO of Apple Computers tomorrow. ❞

— SCOTT ADAMS, *The Joy of Work*

❝ Do not hire a man who does your work for money, but him who does it for the love of it. ❞

— HENRY DAVID THOREAU, *Life Without Principle*

How do companies end up with something like 70 percent of employees that don't even want to be there, let alone produce any results?

The work environment is one likely suspect. But before we go there, let's look at something equally important, but easier to fix: your hiring practices. The fact is, some people are simply wrong for the job. And if you don't know what to look for in a candidate, your hiring decisions are as good as flipping a coin.

To address the issue, we've got to start with building a better matchmaking scheme. One that doesn't reward candidates for gaming the system and is a true test of fit, resonance, passion, belonging, and other such ordinary magic. But before we attempt a solution, let's take a closer look at the problem.

Hiring is hard to do. One, few managers know what they are looking for to begin with. And two, they have no idea who is going to show up for an interview. Even if a résumé has made it through the nine circles of recruiting hell to land on your desk, there's no guarantee that it accurately represents the candidate.

Why? Because people lie on their résumés. If you believe official sources, like this 2012 study by Accu-Screen, Inc., ADP and the Society of Human Resource Managers, they lie a lot:

78% of resumes are "misleading,"
53% of resumes and job applications "contain falsifications,"
33% of resumes have "inaccurate job descriptions,"
29% of resumes "show altered employment dates," and
21% of resumes "state fraudulent degrees."

Does it surprise anyone that a résumé represents a highly jargonized piece of wishful thinking? It shouldn't. Why even write a résumé if it won't tip the scales in your favor?

Some recruiters will try to convince candidates to stick to the facts. They'll say things like, "If you can't get hired without lying, then the job is not for you." But that's exactly the point! Who the hell wants a job they are qualified for? Most people want something way better than they deserve.

This, by the way, is just as true of hiring managers. Aren't we all looking for someone who can do the job of five people and hit the ground running, jumping, and skipping rope? So lying is pretty much built into the system.

The following is a true story of how I got back on my feet after Beauty Co. gave me the boot. It works as well as any to illustrate the bizarre mating ritual we call applying for a job.

At age twenty-three, I was still in college, broke and living in my parents' basement. All my friends had graduated and found good jobs. I decided it was time for me to enjoy the fruits of my education, however incomplete.

Companies were hiring web developers and programmers. There was only one problem: all of them required skills and credentials I did not have. I could have just sent them my résumé, hoping they'd love it so much that they'd forget what they were asking for.

That's what I did the first time around, and—beginner's luck—it worked! However, anywhere outside of rural Pennsylvania, the odds of the hiring manager remembering my high school basketball record were practically nil. Any future employer of mine would go by my résumé, and I'd better make sure it matched what they were after.

This kind of reasoning led me to copy and paste into my résumé every requirement listed for every job my search returned. Not just the flimflam, like "dedicated" and "hardworking," but hard skills: programming languages, operating systems— anything I could find that hiring managers wanted to see on a résumé. I was desperate for paying work, and I wasn't leaving anything up to chance.

Once again, this goes to show you that the gap between one's résumé and one's actual skill set is only limited by one's imagination. Despite what the hiring managers like to believe, no one is qualified for any job on the first day. So why sweat it? My résumé truthfully reflected my willingness to quickly process large amounts of data. But that's where the similarities ended. And it was up to my employer to call my bluff.

A headhunter called me. I put on a tie and a man-bag with nothing in it and went out to meet him at an address in Shartlesville,

Pennsylvania. It turned out to be a shady diner, not much better than a truck stop. I walked in and there he was. A fat old guy in a poop-colored corduroy suit. Dirty Coke-bottle glasses. Bright yellow teeth. I was sure it was a hoax. However, things became quite normal once he started asking questions. These were all typical job interview questions, the kind with the obvious right answers.

> YELLOW TEETH: Have you built enterprise software applications?
> TIM: Absolutely. Buzzword-buzzword-jargon-jargon-lie-lie.

I had been around enterprise solutions enough to know that my intranet project wasn't it. I had coded a bunch of web pages, nothing of the sort of the complex systems architecture he was after. So I didn't dwell on my own exploits and preempted any undue curiosity with a volley of sound bites I had picked up around the office and on the Internet.

That did it for my interviewer. He called me a few days later and told me I'd be working for the Pennsylvania State Treasury Department. The state had just launched tax-sheltered college funds. My job was to put the entire program on the web, so that people could make payments, view their accounts, and produce statements online. It paid $40 an hour.

When I heard that figure, which would put me at $80,000 a year before taxes, I nearly shit my pants. I didn't care if I was leaving any money on the table. I just wanted to get the hell off the phone before the old dude changed his mind.

> TIM: Yes, I can do this. Absolutely.

As I was nodding my head vigorously, technical competency and cultural fit were the last things on my mind. I was thinking more about the two-hour drive each way, to and from Harrisburg, and my course load at Penn State. Thankfully, I was able to transfer to the Harrisburg campus. For the next six months, I would be living off coffee and Howard Stern—but my career was launched and, more importantly, my confidence salvaged.

By the way, I am not telling people to lie to get a job, just in case anyone out there needs my permission. My point is that lying is tempting and easy to get away with. And that it makes it much harder for hiring managers to find the right people.

In fact, hiring is one of the toughest tasks in the workplace. I know, because I routinely ask thousands of people about their biggest challenge at work. Here's a recent crop of responses:

Job Title	Biggest Challenge at Work
President	*"Hiring and keeping good employees"*
Shop Divisional Manager	*"Hiring and retaining good people"*
Managing Director	*"Finding leaders"*

See a pattern?

In my case, the state of Pennsylvania actually did okay on the hiring and the leader part. I did what I was hired to do and saved "the Man" a lot of money. Once again, I pulled all-nighters to get up to speed on the stuff I lied about, and found people and resources to keep me on track and help me learn. The retention part wasn't so good. There was never much other than the paycheck to keep me interested in the job. So, once I figured I could make the same money elsewhere, I left, and the yellow-toothed recruiter was back on the road, hunting for my replacement.

Is there anything companies can do to improve their odds of finding and keeping good leaders? Especially in the face of all the smoke and mirrors that impostors, like myself, put up when they hear the words "job" and "pay"? As it turns out, companies can do a lot. And it has less to do with catching people in their lies, and more with making the lies impossible or irrelevant.

MAKE IT HARDER TO LIE

Let's start by taking a few lies out of the job interview. We have no control over what people put on their résumés, but we have some control over the way they answer our questions. That's because some questions invite lies more than others.

I am thinking about three kinds of questions in particular: (1) Questions that tell people what you want to hear, like "Have you done similar work in the past?" (2) Questions that beg canned responses, like "Tell me about a time you failed." (3) Asking for the impossible.

This last item simply means, understand the scope of the work you're hiring someone to do before you post a wanted ad. When you ask for something that can't be done, you are inviting ignorance and fraud, and closing the door to any qualified help. Unfortunately, this happens more often than we realize. Here's a quick story.

After I left the Pennsylvania State Treasury, I went to work for a startup in California. We were expecting a big round of financing any day. In the meantime, the company often missed payroll. On one of those days, I decided to get a side job.

California was in the middle of a housing bubble. I stumbled upon a one-man mortgage company looking to code a loan-processing interface. He wanted the kind of online application that big players, like LoanDepot, had on their websites. It would take digitizing hundreds of pages of loan docs and coding hundreds of database tables to store the data. I couldn't do it alone. The company couldn't afford it. And even if it could, the housing bubble wouldn't have lasted long enough to justify the cost. In other words, the job was a joke. But it paid $200 an hour, so I took it—and quit after three weeks. The futility of what I was doing crushed me more than the startup roller coaster.

You could point out that I made an asshole of myself, and you would be correct. However, consider that people *always* lie about their abilities and their past, whether they realize it or not. So, anything you can ask of people to *observe them*, rather than take their word, is to your advantage.

So, how do you observe people during a job interview?

Say you were going on a blind date. Do you meet at a coffee shop and take an hour to explain what each of you does for a living and why your last relationship didn't work out? Or ... Advice books say, *do something*, preferably offbeat, on your first date, even if it's a blind one. Why? Because you can learn so much more about people from their response to the unfamiliar than from their doctored life story.

You don't need to take every job candidate on an African safari, but do give them a chance to listen, react, process information, think on their feet, empathize, make decisions, make requests ... In other words, engage in all those activities that, on a very basic level, determine success. Look for spontaneous responses. Any time you exchange canned questions and answers, you are wasting an opportunity to get to know your candidate. Remember, being professional doesn't mean following a script. And if you are one of those people for whom professional means impersonal and robotic, then forget "professional"! Just be yourself and cue the other person to relax and connect with you human-to-human.

A spontaneous off-guard conversation will give you something to observe. Use it to put yourself into the candidate's frame of mind. What motivates him or her? What shuts him down? How does his brain connect the dots? And don't let him off the hook too soon. Ask as many questions as you need to get his thinking. Weigh his responses carefully. Remember that people tend to dwell on precisely those points that they are most insecure about. Someone who uses a lot of technical jargon, like I did, might be worried about sounding incompetent. Someone who harps on taking great care of customers might be worried about coming across as uncaring and self-serving.

According to *The New York Times*, Google hires one hundred people a week to satisfy its need for creative genius. However, less than 1 percent of the geniuses that interview at Google will make the cut. A British newspaper, *The Guardian*, asked Google's one-time SVP of People Operations, Laszlo Bock, how they pick their hires. In the article, "Want to work for Google? Answer these five questions,"[3] he gives a few sample Q&As. Watch how these questions throw the candidate a curveball by making the most obvious answer the wrong one.

"Do you have an IQ higher than 130?" Say "yes," and you have failed the intellectual humility test. Taking your IQ seriously shows that you are looking for ways to prove you are smart, and that's the last thing Google wants you to do.

"What shall we have for dinner this evening?" This one tests for leadership on the spot. Don't beat around the bush. Tell your interviewer what you want to eat or lose him forever.

If you can't take a stand for your favorite dish, can they count on you to give your honest opinion on driverless cars?

"Why did you choose the last five articles you read?" Chances are you have no idea, which is precisely why they ask. They want to see your brain in action. Filter through data quickly to zero in on relevant points. Construct the missing links. Show your work.

"Are you incompetent and lazy?" Answering "yes" to this question gets you into the next round. Incompetence is only a problem when acted upon. Know your limitations.

"Do you have a track record of doing something really well?" If you do, keep it to yourself. Google is a firm believer in beginner's mind. Show that you are willing to look at every problem with a fresh set of eyes.

When I interview someone for a job at Axero, I ask at least one curveball question. It's partly a guilty pleasure and partly a trick to weed out poisonous personalities. One of my favorites is, "What is your drug of choice?" You wouldn't believe the responses I get. Anything from an offended "I don't do drugs" to a dead serious "I like coke every now and then." Both of those would be red flags. But something like, "I did stuff in college, but not anymore" would pass. "I am a workaholic" is too corny for me. But invoking a creative hobby or a sport you actually play is okay.

Zappos has a simple trick for observing job candidates. Here's what CEO Tony Hsieh told *Business Insider*:

> *A lot of our job candidates are from out of town,*
> *and we'll pick them up from the airport in a Zappos*

> *shuttle, give them a tour, and then they'll spend*
> *the rest of the day interviewing, Hsieh says. At the*
> *end of the day of interviews, the recruiter will circle*
> *back to the shuttle driver and ask how he or she*
> *was treated. It doesn't matter how well the day of*
> *interviews went, if our shuttle driver wasn't treated*
> *well, then we won't hire that person.*[4]

It's much easier to foolproof your interviewing strategy if you know what kind of person you want to hire, or, at the very least, what kinds of people you are trying to avoid. Zappos wants nice people who will treat customers like family. Consequently, they worry less about specific job skills and more about *traits* and *behaviors* that give the company its competitive edge—great customer service. You can put whatever you want on your résumé, but if you're a jerk when you think no one's looking, you're not going to get the job.

WHAT'S YOUR COMPANY'S DNA?

Before Zappos, Southwest Airlines had built a successful company on creative customer service. Their motto? *"Hire for attitude, train for skill."* Herb Kelleher, co-founder and former CEO of Southwest Airlines said:

> *We will hire someone with less experience, less*
> *education, and less expertise, than someone who*
> *has more of those things and has a rotten attitude.*
> *Because we can train people. We can teach people*
> *how to lead. We can teach people how to provide*
> *customer service. But we can't change their DNA.*

Genetic or not, certain traits are a must for any position in the company. That's the conclusion these employers have reached after they've asked themselves what it takes for a new hire to make it in the company. Or what it takes to make the company successful, if you want to look at it that way.

For Southwest, it's teamwork, altruism, self-deprecating demeanor, good old work ethic, and "warrior spirit." Sherry Phelps, a top executive in the People Department who spent thirty-three years at Southwest, explains:

> *The first thing we look for is the "warrior spirit." So much of our history was born out of battles—fighting for the right to be an airline, fighting off the big guys who wanted to squash us, now fighting off the low-cost airlines trying to emulate us. We are battle-born, battle-tried people. Anyone we add has to have some of that warrior spirit.*[5]

Accordingly, the company invests in structured interviews and character tests to discover the right people and match them to the jobs. Past experience is no object. Since the airline industry has been consolidating, there's been no shortage of trained flight attendants on the job market. And yet Southwest will hire former teachers, waiters, and police officers that are helpful, caring, and eager, before they hire a veteran flight attendant who is none of those things. How does it pan out? The company admits to a disproportionate selection and training budget, which, they say, pays off in lower turnover, higher productivity, and promotions from within.

For Google, the magic formula is *"general cognitive ability"* (not IQ) plus *"intellectual humility"* plus *"emerging leadership,"* plus *"a sense of ownership to step in and solve any problem"* balanced by *"humility to step back and embrace the better ideas of others."* The test is *"structured behavioral interviews that we validate to make sure they're predictive."*

Google does test its programmers—who make up half of the company—for their ability to write code. Aside from that, Googlers in charge of hiring snub their noses at any conventional measure of competence and success. *The New York Times* reported that, according to Google's Laszlo Bock,

> Google had determined that *"GPAs are worthless as a criteria for hiring, and test scores are worthless.... We found that they don't predict anything ... The proportion of people without any college education at Google has increased over time"*—now as high as 14 percent on some teams.[6]

The point is not to dismiss all formal credentials, but rather to take an unbiased look at which ones make a real difference for your company. If you are like most companies, you over-focus on technical expertise and overlook "soft" skills when you hire people—and you live to regret it. A 2010 study by Leadership IQ says that 46 percent of new hires fail within eighteen months and that 89 percent of these failures are due to poor attitude. Specifically:

> *26% of new hires fail because they can't accept feedback;*
> *23% because they're unable to understand and manage emotions;*
> *17% because they lack the necessary motivation to excel;*
> *15% because they have the wrong temperament for the job;*

*8% because of other problems with attitude; and only
11% of new hires fail because they lack the necessary
technical skills.*

Surprised? Neither are most managers. Eighty-two percent of the 5,247 hiring managers in the study said they had picked up subtle warning signs during the interviews, but hired the candidate anyway because they were too busy, not sure, or too focused on the standard procedure.

How's that for an opportunity?

To be fair, hiring for culture, fit, attitude, or whatever you want to call it, is not all that straightforward. It's much easier to focus on: can this person do the job now? Even for a small company hiring one person, it's not always clear who is going to work out long-term, let alone a huge corporation interviewing hundreds of people every day.

Take my company, for example. I don't have it down to a formula like Google and Southwest. I just know that I like people who have hobbies. If you don't have hobbies, I probably won't hire you. I also like married people—it shows that you can maintain a relationship. I like people with kids—it shows you can handle responsibilities. I like people who hire house cleaners—it shows you care about your surroundings and value your time. These are pretty basic ideas, but they give me a sense of comfort about who will be doing my work when I am not there.

BE WILLING TO MAKE EXCEPTIONS

When you don't know what defines a great candidate, you might defer to your intuition. This is particularly true of small companies who don't have the budget for structured behavioral interviews.

When I hired people in the past, I used to rely on my gut feel and my pet interview questions, no exceptions. And I would have told you to do the same. But, if I had followed my own advice a few years ago, I would have never hired Bryce. And, without him, our company wouldn't be what it is today. In fact, without Bryce, we might not have a company at all.

Bryce found us when we weren't looking. He was willing to do whatever we threw at him—for next to nothing. How do you turn down someone like that? After a month or two of working remotely, I invited Bryce to come out to San Diego to spend a week face-to-face. I decided he should stay with me, to save on the hotel and maximize our time together. He accepted. Neither of us knew what we were in for.

It started with our trip to Costco. After I picked Bryce up from the airport, I took him grocery shopping. Thinking to treat him to a home-cooked meal, I headed straight for the fresh produce aisle.

> TIM: What do you like to eat, Bryce?
> BRYCE: Um … whatever.
> TIM: No, seriously. We're here to buy food. Any kind of food. What do you want?
> BRYCE: Uh … um … well … I tend to stick with what I'm used to.
> TIM: What are you used to?
> BRYCE: Um … I could do Hot Pockets.
> TIM: Hot Pockets?? Sure, Bryce. Hot Pockets it is!

Bryce was clearly no New Age health nut. So much for my world-famous vitamin-packed breakfast smoothies! Luckily,

San Diego has an endless variety of food. I was sure I could find something that both of us liked to eat.

For lunch, I took Bryce for a hamburger and a beer at Yard House, a spot about as American as you get without singing the Anthem. As soon as the waiter brought out the menus, I knew I was way off again. Neither the sweet potato fries nor the local brews turned him on. Bryce endured half of a grilled chicken sandwich and flat-out refused any alcohol. So much for letting loose over a couple of beers.

The social program was an even bigger flop than the meal plan. One of the nights, I invited some friends over and rented *Pirates of Silicone Valley*. Eighty-nine percent Rotten Tomatoes. Plus, who wouldn't like to see the dirt on Steve Jobs and Bill Gates for the *n*th time? My friends unanimously approved my pick. Bryce politely sat through the movie—with his back to the TV. He was hard at work, while the rest of us were killing time in his honor.

Nature didn't do any better than culture.

> TIM: Wanna go to the beach, Bryce?
> BRYCE: Sounds reasonable.
> TIM: What did you think of the cliffs, Bryce?
> BRYCE: They're nice.
> TIM: Just nice?
> BRYCE: Quite nice?

At this moment, Tim the Artist had a heated argument with Tim the Businessman. The artist demanded Bryce be fired on the spot for his lack of appreciation of Tim's spectacular talents.

EXHIBIT 1: Tim's spectacular cooking skills.

EXHIBIT 2: Tim's spectacular sense of humor, as evident in his choice of films.

EXHIBIT 3: Tim's spectacular choice of tourist attractions, the incomparable Sunset Cliffs.

I was willing to write off Bryce's taste in food and movies as his own private affair. But the cliffs were the last straw. Sunset Cliffs Natural Park is a national treasure chock-full of jaw-dropping, camera-clicking tourists all year around. If he was going to be so damn hard to impress, then the hell with him. I'd rather work with someone who likes the same things I do.

Luckily, my partner, Vivek, intervened. Bryce safely returned home to Kansas with his job intact. Pretty soon, he made himself indispensable as customer support and at just about every other job in the company. He was as caring and helpful on the phone, as he had seemed withdrawn and uptight in person. He was always there for anything and everything the customer needed. He even learned programming, so he could create new features and fix bugs. In the days when Vivek and I worried ourselves sick about landing new business, Bryce was the last man standing to hold down the fort for customers.

He is still with us today, and I humbly beg his forgiveness for my test of fit. I hope this story will save some budding entrepreneur from the biggest mistake of his career. Learn everything you can about culture and attitude, but please remember to always make an exception for amazing people like Bryce.

And here's the thing about judging other people's attitude. You come face-to-face with your own. Why couldn't I see how patient, open-hearted, and courageous he was to leave his quiet home in Kansas and come to loud and pretentious San Diego? Why was I trying so hard to conquer him with my hospitality?

Bryce changed the way I hire people. It's no longer about my gut response. It's about the contribution they could make to the company I am building. And, as far as that goes, an interview, no matter how well thought out, is simply not the best way to tell. Anything you can do to try your candidates out in the real world will get you closer to your dream team.

So what does that look like in practice?

Whole Foods gives every new hire a ninety-day trial. After that, the entire team votes the newbie in or out.

Zappos starts every job with four weeks of training. That includes two weeks in the call center. Tony Hsieh put himself through the first training, and every Zappos employee, from execs to the kitchen staff, has done the same ever since. One reason every new hire has to do the call center is that everyone works the phones during the holiday season. The other reason is a chance to get real. *"It's pretty hard to fake your way through that entire four weeks,"* says Tony.

Besides firing people who fail the training, Zappos does something very odd to foolproof the rest. They offer every new hire $4,000—eight weeks' pay for an average hourly employee— to quit before training is over. Tony says about 2 percent take the buyout—a small price to pay for true love.

Behind any successful hiring strategy is the simple fact that you need to get real about two things: (1) who shows up to the job interview, and (2) what it takes to do the job. Get good at both of these, and you've mastered the matchmaking game.

What's next? Will "employee engagement" take care of itself from here on out? Not quite. Now it's time for the company to get real about how it puts the new hire to work.

CHAPTER 3
ENGAGE FROM DAY ONE

❝Four years ago I was hired as a consultant. I was told there was an incredible number of projects waiting to be done. I sat there for three weeks before I figured out that there was no work to do.❞

— SCOTT ADAMS, *The Joy of Work*

❝Start with what is right rather than what is acceptable.❞

— FRANZ KAFKA

I landed my internship with Beauty Co. after two summers at a Coke bottling plant, four months of selling Persian rugs at a farmers market, a year as an electrician's apprentice, seven months of fitting cheap glasses at a local optometrist's, and countless days and nights of waiting tables. To say I was excited is to say nothing at all.

Even though I despised every job I'd ever had, I was convinced that life in corporate IT would be different. Finally, a company thought highly enough of me to trust me to do important things I was learning at school. I was proud to wear long sleeves and long pants on a hot summer day. Thrilled to step inside a cubicle wasteland. Eager to be stuffed into a dusty corner, away from fresh air and sunlight. It was *the first day of my future as a professional.*

The company gave me a lukewarm reception. People seemed too busy to pay attention to a dorky khaki-blue creature sheepishly peeking into their cubicles. I felt intimidated by everyone I met. Later, when I found out exactly how my coworkers kept themselves busy, I understood why they didn't welcome me with open arms. Company business occupied a small fraction of their time. They were afraid that, in my youthful zeal, I'd blow their cover—or worse, do actual work and make them look bad. Accordingly, they treated me like a resident leper until I was properly initiated into the office routine.

That didn't take long. On my first day, I got paired up with another PC tech for on-the-job training. My first task was to install Napster on my PC and download as many songs as fast as I could. Napster was under a federal court injunction, and it was a matter of days before it would shut down.

With the combined manpower of the entire IT team (minus management), we were able to download thousands of songs every day. The network, overwhelmed with incoming MP3s, slowed down to a crawl, causing loud complaints from every direction. Of course, most people's jobs didn't require an outside connection. They needed it to watch movies, shop or play games online—and were understandably upset with the delays.

We felt their pain and asked management for a faster connection. Our request was promptly granted, thanks, no doubt, to some high-ranking online-movie lovers. We got a full T1 connection with optic fibers, the fastest at the time. This was my first lesson in the power of IT to ease suffering and bring joy to people at work.

Even though it helped me discover my life's calling, on the whole, my internship was a letdown. There was no training to speak of. When I got a network error message, I was told to go Google it. I felt like an idiot, until I figured out that everyone there was flying by the seat of their pants. My boss was an idiot. My boss's boss was an idiot. The rank-and-file IT people were not much better technology-wise, but they had discovered a way to game the system, so that the management would rely on them for day-to-day decisions.

It wasn't long before I realized that I owed my job to ignorance and fraud, rather than to my superior credentials and boyish charm. My second task, after Napster, was to walk around with a Microsoft Office Update CD and run security patches on every computer. *Huh?* Even I knew that the Systems Administrator could simultaneously install software updates on all networked PCs without leaving his desk. I asked my trainer why we had to go around. "We turned the automatic updates off," he explained, "so that we can get away from our desks and look busy."

In the weeks that followed I got excellent training in make-believe work. The manual updates took days, if not weeks. It wasn't just getting to everyone's desk. Once I got there, people tried every trick in the book to shoo me away.

"I don't have time right now."

"I don't need it."

"I don't use my PC that much."

"Who are you, again?"

It was useless to explain security patches. People are naturally skilled at what one IT director described as, "being intentionally dense with technology." Besides, they didn't want anyone near their computers for fear of being caught doing exactly what we were doing—wasting time. So I had to lie in wait for them to go to the bathroom or even stay after-hours to finish my make-believe assignments.

Sometimes people from the hair salons called with computer problems. They were actually busy cutting hair. There was no way they would stand there and listen to self-troubleshooting instructions over the phone. They wanted me to come over and fix it for them. Another outstanding opportunity to waste time! Instead of calling the computer shop next door, I'd get in the car and drive one hundred miles each way to yank hair out of a computer fan.

When we didn't feel like dealing with fellow humans, we'd go hide in the server room. You could open a screen window and sit in front of the server for hours, looking like you were working. Or you could go into the "cage," a fenced graveyard for spare parts. You'd take out a few broken mice and dirty keyboards and act like you were building a space shuttle. If anyone dared question you, you made sure he felt like an idiot.

> MANAGER: What are you doing?
> IT GUY: Fixing a computer.
> MANAGER: What are you doing that for?
> IT GUY: It doesn't work.

The IT department was so good at looking busy that it took not one, but two interns that summer. The second intern was none other than the owner's son. There was a lot of tiptoeing around him, until he, too, soaked in our ways and became one of us. He was wasting his father's money for no reason other than that everyone else was doing it. That's the true power of culture! (More about that in Chapter 16.)

I am not telling you all this because I am holding a mean grudge against Beauty Co. On the contrary, I am grateful to them for having launched my career. I told you this story because, in one way or another, every one of my jobs started just like my internship: with frustrated enthusiasm and general disappointment.

Yes, life is often frustrating and disappointing. What can you do?

The first thing to do is to realize that new hires are special. Even if you have a roomful of disgruntled employees chewing up the company's time and thanklessly collecting paychecks, you get a free pass every time you hire a new one. People are silly creatures. No matter how many times they get burned, they hold out hope for the next time. The next diet will be a miracle. The next boyfriend won't be a jerk. The next girlfriend won't be psycho. The next job will make me into a rock star.

With every new hire, you get a bit of free curiosity, enthusiasm, good intentions, a beginner's mind ... These are some of the best attitudes you can hope for in an employee. Can you hold on to them and put them to work? You can, if you act fast.

This is not so much about having a formal welcoming procedure. It's about detecting whether what you are doing—or not doing—for your new hires is helping or hurting them. Not giving it any thought whatsoever is probably not going to help. But there are many alternatives, from very formal to completely casual.

Formal new hire orientations are in, especially with big employers with expansive HR departments. Each program is unique, but many contain the following three elements. Here they are, along with some points to consider.

CULTURAL IMMERSION

Wherever groups of humans spend significant time together, a culture spontaneously emerges. This will happen with or without the approval and participation of corporate HR, and there is nothing anyone can do to keep a new hire from dipping a toe in it. Some will plunge in and thrive. Others will hold back and languish.

A thorough hiring scheme can minimize this latter group, but not eliminate it entirely. As we've seen, no test of fit is as good as the job itself. So, as much as we'd like to use the orientation to wed each newly selected employee to the company, it's smarter to make it easy for them to back out.

Think of the orientation as a self-selection phase, not a brainwashing tool. Make it as *real* as possible, without hazing the newbies. Recall Zappos' new-hire training. There is wisdom in having it be the last chance to fail and give up the spot to someone who truly deserves it. Let the new people see how your business functions and what the job is really like. If they're going to hate it, it's better to realize it early on and give them a no-hard-feelings escape route.

Here's another company that has thought through the immersion phase. USAA is an insurance carrier *"serving those who serve,"* the U.S. military and their families exclusively. It handles banking, insurance, and other financial needs of the troops and the vets. It even helps them sell houses and pick out engagement rings.

You don't have to be a veteran to work at USAA, but you do need to know something about the military. And, although there is no real way to walk in their shoes, unless you are one of them, the orientation helps. During your first week on the job, you will try on combat gear. You will have MREs (Meals Ready to Eat, also known as Meals Ready to Excrete and Meals Rejected by Ethiopians) for lunch. The point is, obviously, not to give you a world-class culinary experience, but to open your heart to compassion and gratitude. You will also receive an authentic deployment letter, just to see what might be going on in the background while your customer is shopping for life insurance or investing his life's savings.

Notice something highly unusual about this program. USAA immersion week is not really about USAA. It's about the customers. Its goal is nothing short of crossing the barriers between the military and civilian life, which, when you think about it, is the company's whole reason for being. Under these circumstances, a formal introduction into the culture is necessary. It also works.

MISSION, VISION, AND VALUES

Should you drill your new hires in corporate propaganda?

Maybe. But consider the delivery as carefully as you do the content. A boring presentation on the corporate mission, vision, and values will only convince the new hire that the company is useless, narcissistic, and doesn't value his time.

Even a cool company can save most of its cute and funny folklore for the after-hours. Zappos publishes an annual *Culture Book* for that purpose. Inside is *"a collage of unedited submissions from employees within the Zappos Family of companies sharing what the Zappos culture means to them."* People say nice things like, *"The Zappos culture means never feeling awkward around anyone you don't know ..."* or *"It's hard to have a bad day ..."* or an ambitious, *"We are the social engineers of our time."*

A British software company, Redgate, wordcrafts *The Book of Redgate*, *"to capture the mysterious essence of the Redgate brand"* and *"to help new Redgaters absorb some of our culture."* The book contains thirteen guiding principles (*number 4 is, Don't be an asshole*), an advice column (*Ask the Vending Machine*), stories about work, food, sabbaticals, etc., a crossword puzzle, and lots of the color red.

Bottom line: if your mission, vision and values are a mere formality, then skip it! There is a reason why many companies are treading these subjects lightly—they have nothing to say. Not yet, anyway. Skip ahead to Chapter 21 if you need emergency assistance discovering your company's mission.

However, if you truly are on a mission, you probably want your people to take it as close to the heart as you do. What is the best way to reach them? Is it a personal story? Crowdsourcing? Humor? Aim for a strong connection. And, whatever form it takes, remember to check in with your people to see whether it makes a difference in their daily work.

MINDLESS PAPERWORK

Being new means filling out forms and creating passwords. Ideally, it should be done beforehand. Why crowd out the excitement of the first day with mind-numbing activities? You know how they tell you that the first few hours of your morning are best for accomplishing the most important task of the day? The same goes for the first time a person sets foot at a job.

Which begs the question: what are the most important things for the new hire to do? If the above list didn't inspire you, try these instead:

MEET THE MAN BEHIND THE LEGEND

Facebook is not necessarily Mark Zuckerberg, but spending time with the founder does something to help the new hire see the possibilities. *The New York Times* reports that Zuckerberg likes to make his job offers in person while taking the candidate for a walk through the woods.

If your company is virtual or spread over many locations, this might be your people's only chance to get to know you as a person. Do it sooner rather than later. Danny Wegman, the CEO of Wegmans Food Markets (no. 12 on *Fortune's* "100 Best Companies to Work For" in 2014), has chartered jets to fly all new full-time employees to Rochester, N.Y. for a face-to-face welcome. About.me, a personal webhosting service founded in 2009, flies all the new hires to San Francisco for beer and sausage.

SHARE THE SPOTLIGHT

Companies don't need to drone on about how great they are any more than people. A better strategy is to let the new hires do the talking—says a study of 605 employees of Wipro, a business process outsourcing firm, located in New Delhi, India. During the orientation, managers asked people to talk about their strengths, for example, to describe a time when they felt "born to act." As a welcome gift, the study subjects got sweatshirts imprinted with their own names, not the company's. These new hires were up to 32 percent less likely to quit within six months, compared to those who sat through a typical company-centered talk[7].

FREE STUFF

Gifts are a time-honored way to make people feel welcome. If gold, frankincense, and myrrh are not your company's specialty, then aim for something closer to home. These are just some examples:

Twitter gives each new hire a bottle of wine. Airbnb, a site that lets you rent rooms from individuals around the world, gives incoming employees $2,000 to spend on travel. Dropbox showers them with free online storage.

UNIQUE, WEIRD, AND DOWNRIGHT INSULTING

LinkedIn greets new hires with a card that says, "You are [In]." New Amazon employees get a desk made out of an old door. (They used to have to make their own, but now it comes pre-assembled.) Apple employees have to set up their own brand-new iMac on their first day. Rackspace starts people off with four days of games, skits, music, and a limbo bar. New Googlers have to wear silly hats that say *Noogler* to their first Friday all-hands meeting.

ASK THE EMPLOYEE

I wouldn't recommend the item directly above, unless you are freaking Google and can afford to haze your new hires. At the other extreme, if you want to make every dollar count, why not ask your people what would make their job easy? All of my employees work remotely, so I routinely help them set up their workspaces. I've paid for high-speed Internet, cell phones, computers, software. Occasionally, even a housecleaner—as I've told you, I believe in housecleaners. Training is another popular request. We send people to conferences and workshops to get better at whatever it is they do for us.

MAKE FRIENDS

Introduce your new hires to people around the office. Ask them to make a list of everyone in the company they need to know in order to do their jobs well. Have them start building relationships with people on their lists within the first two weeks. If you have a social intranet, connect the new hire and let him browse profiles and conversations before his start date.

Google uses orientations to help new hires connect with each other. They found out that group size makes a difference. People who went through the orientation in groups of twelve were more comfortable and formed closer ties than those in larger groups.

SCORE A QUICK WIN

Here's a novel idea: put your new hire to work. *The Wall Street Journal* reports that new developers at the dog-boarding site Rover.com make live updates on the company's website on their first day. It's helped new people build confidence, and it makes the rest of the troops pick up the pace to have everything ready before the new employee arrives.

Getting a project completed on day one may be too ambitious, especially for teams. Give the new hire a small but important first challenge and see how quickly he can get results. I like to see something within the first week or two.

SET EXPECTATIONS

Can your new hire set and keep a deadline? This step is mundane, but crucial, especially for small companies, like Axero, who don't have a lot of room for error. In my business, people routinely underestimate the time it takes to do everything—who doesn't?

I've learned the hard way to ask, "Are you sure you don't need another week? Month?"

Are your new hires open and direct, or do they hide their tracks and dance around issues? Can we solve problems on the spot, or do we need to schedule everything? Do they waste time? I check in often at first, not to tell them what to do, but to make sure things are as they seem.

How you talk is important. I like to relax and cut through formalities. I'll swear, if I have to. One time I accidentally said, "fuck," in front of a new hire. I thought I'd messed up, but he was thrilled—instant bonding. You can't always count on it, of course, but you'd be surprised how many problems get solved when you give up your act and start being yourself.

To make it really simple, how do you get your new hires to aim high, pay attention to detail, cut out the bull, take interest in people, and generally make you happy?

Do it to them first.

There is no better way than practicing what you preach.

From day one.

CHAPTER 4
SET GOALS

" … I copied Wally's line, 'I streamlined my business processes while honing my participatory style and my proactive attitude, all while valuing diversity,' into my description of work in the review. My pointy haired boss either didn't see the humor in it or didn't read it at all and it is now part of my permanent record as an employee. **"**

— SCOTT ADAMS, *The Joy of Work*

" Give me a stock clerk with a goal and I'll give you a man who will make history. Give me a man with no goals and I'll give you a stock clerk. **"**

— J.C. PENNEY

Goals are akin to desires—and even an amateur Buddhist will tell you that desires are the root of all suffering. The pleasure of an accomplished goal is shallow and fleeting, but the pressure of a goal-driven life is everlasting.

So, why bother with goals? Here's why. Your employees— even the Buddhist ones—are human, and as such, are subject to goals and desires of their own. Therefore, misery in the workplace cannot be completely eliminated. However, it can be minimized if we take care to match up individual goals and aspirations to those of the company.

We will talk about company-wide goals later. For now, let's just assume that they exist and make sense, and that the company is motivated to achieve them. In this case, employees need to stay in the loop and set individual goals to enable the common goal.

This must not be as obvious as it sounds, because companies are full of people who go through the motions of their jobs without getting the bigger picture. According to a 2014 About.com poll, the top cause of disengagement at work is "*lack of direction from management,*" accounting for 38 percent of all responses.

One more stat from BlessingWhite 2013 *Employee Engagement Research Update*: 20 percent of employees chose "*greater clarity about what the organization needs me to do—and why*" as the item that would most improve their performance. Another 20 percent chose "*more resources.*" These two answers tied for the top factor influencing employee contribution globally.

However, when it comes to engaging people, greater clarity wins over all other options (including more and better feedback, development opportunities, mentoring, communicating with the boss, and relationships with coworkers). Almost a third of the disenchanted employees and 28 percent of those totally disengaged said they could improve, given clearer goals.

So, what's stopping them?

"Management" is an easy answer. Managers are infinitely skilled at confusing and alienating people. But I am getting ahead of myself. We will talk about managers and their relationships with their direct reports in Part Two: *Empower the Relationship*. For now, let's look at the different ways we let people lose their "line of sight." I have personally made all of these mistakes and will make many more before I step down. The good part is that, if you recognize yourself in even one of these scenarios, you can turn it around and start getting radically different results from the same people.

MISTAKE #1: SET NO GOALS

Employee goals are the link between the success of the company and what people do day to day. When this link is secure, strategies are executed, and any strategic flaws are reported up the chain. When this link is weak, reduced to a formality, or completely missing, the strategy falls flat on its face. In hindsight, we might say it was a bad idea—or blame some nebulous engagement factor—when, in fact, many people simply didn't know that it was up to them to make the effort. They thought it was somebody else's job.

I learned this lesson back in our startup days, when Vivek and I decided to hire interns. We had heard from other startups that it was a fun and low-cost way to cut down our dreary to-do lists. Apparently, some interns out there were so good that they added features and launched products in between their regular chores.

It hadn't been long since my own stint as an intern at Beauty Co. I remembered how excited I was to get out of sucky summer jobs and do something "professional." I thought I'd give the same chance to as many kids as I could fit into a small room. We rented office space downtown and proudly installed two interns: one boy and one girl. Having been in their shoes once, I thought I knew exactly how to handle interns. There would be no micromanagement. The projects were all laid out in the system. The interns could jump right in—or even create their own.

Well, that's not what happened. Our two Cinderellas craved micromanagement. And, unless I was there to administer it in heavy doses, nothing would ever get done. Most days I didn't make it to the office, so the office space was a complete waste. I shut it down and told the interns to work from home. That's when the work stopped altogether, and the Axero Summer Internship Program was effectively terminated.

I was so pissed that, for several years after, Axero didn't hire interns. Then I let Bryce handle it, and—wow, what a difference! Now we have happy, productive interns all the time. It dawned on me that I had messed up the first two because I never took the time to learn what they wanted out of their jobs. Nor did I ever explain how they could make a difference for the company. Devoid of a context and personal interest, the job came down to meaningless and confusing tasks.

Why wouldn't I see to it that the interns had clear and important goals to accomplish? Sometimes, the hardest to see are the things we think are obvious. I knew what my goals were, and it didn't occur to me that the interns needed help setting theirs. Without goals to reach, work becomes business as usual—in their case, sitting around waiting for the boss to show up. I am convinced that most of the dreaded resistance to change in the workplace is nothing but poorly understood individual goals.

MISTAKE #2: MAKE IT TOO EASY

A popular variation on Set No Goals are goals that take no extra effort—something to put in the performance plan and forget for the rest of the year. These goals are not so much a slam-dunk—we salute the slam-dunks if they are a step in the new direction—as they are already part of the routine. Not only do you not have to strive to achieve them, you don't even have to think to put them down. These kinds of goals, although clear and consistent, do not live up to their name.

Unlike the boring routine goals, exciting motivational goals bring out a sense of *success*—an intrinsic motivator our minds obey in any setting. Leadership IQ surveyed 5,000 workers in various fields to study the impact of goal-setting on employee engagement. They found that people who set motivational goals are up to 75 percent more fulfilled than people who set routine goals.

In his book, *HARD Goals*, Leadership IQ founder Mark Murphy makes a case for goals that are (a) heartfelt or emotionally appealing; (b) animated by dreams and a vision; (c) required or necessary and urgent; and (d) difficult or developmental, outside of the comfort zone.

In other words, in order to motivate, a performance goal needs to be a true goal, something our heart desires, but doesn't yet have within easy reach.

MISTAKE #3: MAKE IT TOO HARD

That said, don't set your sights too high too soon. It's true that high expectations bring people out of their comfort zones. It is also true that unrealistic goals lead to quick disappointment and burnout. A case in point is El Cheapo Vision Center.

The day I quit the electrician apprenticeship, I drove to Penn State and reenrolled myself full-time. I had no more illusions about making a living by the sweat of my brow, but the next semester was six months away, and I needed a job to tide me over.

El Cheapo Vision Center was hiring "opticians." We wore white lab coats and fitted glasses. But our real job was to sell.

The store lured in customers with cheap frames, and we were to upsell them into polycarbonate lenses, anti-glare coatings, and color contacts. The job only paid a minimum wage, but they told us that we could double it … if we met our targets.

The sales targets came down from the corporate. Managers posted them daily on big dry-erase boards. The problem was that nobody hit them. Ever. The targets exceeded our normal throughput by an order of magnitude. If we sold five pairs of glasses a day, the targets called for fifty.

The ridiculous targets left people with two options: (1) quit your job or (2) resign yourself to the fact that you were never going to make any money. The permanent staff whittled itself down accordingly. It consisted of a manager raising six kids over the office phone and an optician with eyesight so bad he couldn't read the prescriptions. The rest were a rotating band of juvenile delinquents equally cynical towards the goals and the job itself.

We came to work stoned and hung over. We served ourselves first. And, since the store neglected to give us employee discounts, we had to set them up ourselves. Something easy to calculate, like 100 percent off anything that fit into a lab coat pocket.

Despite everyone's best efforts to the contrary, El Cheapo had lots of customers. These were the unfortunate souls who relied on glasses for their daily living, myself included. Suddenly left without, they had no choice but to drive up to the nearest dump that sold glasses.

One day a guy came in sweating profusely.

> SWEATY CUSTOMER: I broke my glasses. I need a replacement.
>
> TIM: Absolutely. Are you okay?

SWEATY CUSTOMER: I have malaria.

TIM: Right. Let me get someone else to help you.

Just a few minutes at the store would have convinced anyone that we didn't want any customers. But the people who set our sales targets never came by. Those same people also sent us lists of past customers to cold-call. This was the one task the delinquents embraced. You'd go into a room by yourself and shut the door. For the next few hours you'd have the exclusive use of a desk, a comfortable chair, a phone, and a computer to do whatever pleased your young imaginative soul. One minute before the end of your shift, you'd put check marks next to a few dozen names. Then you'd hand the list back to your manager and say, "These people don't want anything."

Unachievable goals are demoralizing. Aim for a stretch, not a strain, and keep in mind that these will vary from one individual to the next. Test the ground with reasonable goals and let the employee demonstrate that he is ready for more. It's better to build on a small success than on a spectacular failure.

"TELLING IS NOT SELLING"

Another lesson from El Cheapo's failed sales strategy is that the company's target is not automatically an employee's goal. Telling people what you want them to achieve is not enough. You have to "sell" them on the commitment. The first three letters in Mark Murphy's HARD goals are about emotional attachment, urgency and meaning. Only the D is for "difficult" or "hard."

Should goals be HARD, SMART, CLEAR, some combination of—or none of the above? Goal setting is an art, which explains why every third motivational speaker has a revolutionary new acronym. All I know is that, when done right, goal setting is extremely powerful. You just have to know what works for you and for the people you are trying to manage. Look back at a time when you set and achieved a goal. Here's mine:

After I took the state treasury job in Harrisburg, I would wake up at 5:30 every morning and drive two hours to work. I'd leave work at 5:00 p.m. and go to class from 6:00 to 9:00 p.m. Drive home from 9:00 to 11:00 p.m. And, since I lied on my resume and didn't know squat about building interactive websites, I would study into the wee hours of the morning. Then I'd go to bed, only to repeat the cycle in less than four hours.

Doesn't sound like the pothead who fitted glasses at El Cheapo, does it? What happened?

Well, let's eliminate some possibilities. Was I working for a better company? Not necessarily. The Pennsylvania State Treasury was no Googleplex. To change one field in the database, I had to track down a network administrator in a different part of the building, put in a request to get a login to a server, then sit on my hands for days while my request was "being processed."

Did I have a better team? Not unless working alone is your idea of a great team. During my six months at the state treasury, I saw my manager three times. Once when he hired me, once when I quit, and once when I accidentally bumped into him walking down the hall. I tried to get help from people around me. I asked the contractor in the cubicle next to mine who was the best person to answer my questions. He told me to take a look around.

"Do you see anyone working?" he asked.

This was a rhetorical question, implying that everyone around us was twiddling their thumbs, just like my Beauty Co.'s coworkers during my phony security updates.

"These are all union employees," he said. "They don't do any work, because they can't lose their jobs. That's why the government hires contractors."

Whether or not it was as bad as all that, I took him at his word. And that was that for teamwork and collaboration.

What else was different? The money certainly helped, but it doesn't explain why I worked equally hard on Beauty Co.'s intranet and a broke startup in California. What these jobs had and others didn't was an ambitious target that was up to me to hit or miss. It was the difference between working towards a goal and trading time for a paycheck. I was also completely sold on and committed to my goals—something no amount of money can guarantee. Here's what I believe did it for me:

1. **I could see the finished product in my mind's eye.** An easy to use, well thought out website. Something that actually helped people accomplish important tasks. The more I worked on it, the more ideas I had, and the more I wanted to see them through.

2. **I could see myself vastly better off for completing the project.** Accomplishing my goal meant being able to afford a place of my own. It meant never again cleaning other people's eyeglasses and pulling hair out of computers. It also meant proving it to myself that I could do it. Confidence doesn't grow on trees, you know?

3. **I was drawn to the work.** I started with a few simple web pages and moved on to e-commerce, user experience, graphics, all the way to complex collaborative spaces Axero does now. With every

success, I naturally wanted to continue along the same path. I wasn't forcing myself to go to work for the sake of money or recognition. I would do it with or without.

If you can set and achieve your own goals, you are ready to help others. And a lot of people out there need help. The 2013 *Trends in Global Employee Engagement* report by Aon Hewitt lists *performance management* as the second top driver of employee engagement in North America (after career opportunities).

You already know that you can't set anyone else's goals—because everything that makes a goal stick varies from one individual to the next. What you *can* do is give coaching and support. Make the company and team goals clear. Set expectations. Then let people set their own goals, the kind that inspire ownership and commitment. Ask them to use simple and direct language that has specific meaning.

A little bit of coaching skill in this area goes a long way. So, let's talk about how goals work in general, the ones that do, anyway. Then you can help your people set goals that work *for* them and not *against* them.

Any goal they can possibly choose will fall into one of three categories: (1) something they've done before; (2) something they haven't done, but others have; and (3) something no one's ever done before.

In the first case, they more or less know what they need to do to be successful. The goal easily converts to a set of tasks or to-do lists. (Eventually, any goal must come down to a to-do list, so "easily" is the key word.) From there, it's a matter of sticking to their priorities. And here, again, "too easy" or risk-free doesn't cut it, because our priorities usually come from goals of a higher order.

Goals of the third kind are like world peace, eradicating cancer, or vacationing on another planet. Although highly motivating, they have no time horizon and, therefore, are useless as performance targets. They are, however, invaluable as timeless missions bringing people together inside and outside the company. We'll talk about this at length later on.

This leaves us with number two—things we haven't done ourselves, but have seen other people do. An athlete setting a personal record. Facebook going to China. Who-the-hell-is-Tim-Eisenhauer writing a business advice book. The middle category of goals fills the spectrum between the probable and the possible. Most big goals people set for themselves fall into this category. And, for the reasons we've just discussed, they certainly should. These are also the kinds of goals people shy away from when it comes to their jobs. Why risk failing and looking ridiculous?

So, how do you motivate your people to set ambitious goals?

First, find something important to them. A heartfelt goal disrupts our usual, habitual, automatic way of thinking. And ... whoa! We see and act on the possibilities that have escaped us before. Are they already working on a new project or learning a new skill? That's excellent proof that they care. Make sure the new project serves the entire team, then—

Second, give it your full and public support. Put your own commitment behind the goal, so that the risks are shared. Goals arise in the world of imagination and possibilities—frequently one person's world. If successful, they make their way into material existence—a world shared by many. The more other people share in our beliefs, the more likely it is that the goal will pull through the invisible barrier separating the real from the imaginary.

Finally, remind them that goals have a miraculous power to direct our lives. Author J. D. Salinger was among the 3,080 soldiers of the 12th U.S. Infantry Regiment who landed on Utah Beach on D-Day, June 6, 1944. By the end of June, his regiment had lost about 2,500 men. Salinger, who was working on a novel he had begun in 1941, survived. He carried the first six chapters with him throughout the war. *The Catcher in the Rye* was published in 1951. It became one of the best-known works of the twentieth century. Salinger believed that the unfinished novel had saved his life.

We will never know what saved Salinger. But one thing is for certain: in the midst of the very real scenes of death and carnage, he had a vision of his finished work. And that vision eventually became his reality.

Today, people visualize all kinds of things, from quitting smoking to time travel. They believe that detailed imagery will bring them closer to their goals. I can't say that I am a devout visualizer, but I did experiment with it once. I took a screenshot of my bank account and Photoshopped it to show $1,000,000. Very poetic, I know. Anyway, it did do something to move it from a "dream'" to a "goal." And I have never doubted that I will achieve it, ever since.

Along with inspiration, goals can bring disappointment and worry. "What if I don't make it?" "What if I'm not good enough?" This is where your coaching makes a difference. Acknowledge your employees' past achievements. Help them visualize success. Recommend an inspirational book. If nothing else, they give all of us a break from negativity.

TWEAK YOUR TOOLS

Just as goals are personal to the employee, performance management systems are unique to the company. Question your process and customize your tools. This is how one company does it.

In January of 2011, Motorola, Inc. spun off its consumer cell phone operation and changed its name to Motorola Solutions. One year later, the company reformed its performance review protocol. Among other things, they got rid of ratings. Shelly Carlin, Motorola's senior vice president of human resources, believed the ratings became an obstacle to employee engagement:

> *In the old system, managers sat in judgment of another adult. By nature, that setup breeds tension. Employees won't be open to feedback because they'll want to defend their livelihood. We knew we would never completely eliminate the power differential in that relationship, but we wanted to encourage managers to ask questions of self-discovery. Most employees don't come to work wanting to do a bad job. They want to contribute, advance, and grow. Managers should be all about helping them do that.*[8]

Next, the paperwork moved to the cloud, so that corporate HR could simultaneously reach all employees around the globe. That's where the uniformity ended. The new system set the local managers free to do what worked best in each individual case. Now a manager may meet monthly with one employee, but only twice a year with another. Carlin believes that *"performance management isn't a series of checkpoints. It should be much more fluid and customized than that."* The goal is to train the managers to know when and how to intervene.

A worthy goal indeed. Many companies have been working on individualized performance management for years, Axero among them. We even came close once. Our secret was to shrink the company from thirty people to eight. At the time, we flat-out couldn't performance-manage thirty people.

Like Motorola, we no longer use a series of checkpoints to drop in on our people. It's more like one continuous checkpoint. We pair our developers together, so they can talk about the code they are writing beforehand and critique it afterwards. We learned that the extra planning step saves time down the road: people are writing better software faster.

On a very basic level, setting and achieving goals comes down to two things: attention and intention. Intention is your desired outcome. We've talked it back and forth in this chapter—what it means in the context of your job and what it does to open opportunities. The next chapter is about what it takes to close on those opportunities.

Can you focus your attention and keep your eyes on the prize?

CHAPTER 5
KEEP THE EYES ON THE PRIZE

“ I don't care how much power, brilliance or energy you have,
if you don't harness it and focus it on a specific target, and
hold it there, you're never going to accomplish as much as
your ability warrants. ”

— ZIG ZIGLAR

You've heard the Rolling Stones: you can't always get what you want. Sometimes goals work, and sometimes they malfunction. How meticulously we set them has nothing to do with it. Smart, clear, convincing and realistic goals blow up in our faces all the time.

You can vocalize and visualize your goals. You can put them in writing and broadcast them to the world. You can break them into steps and enter them into your performance plan. You can do all that without moving any closer to your goals.

Surprised?

Of course not. A goal is little more than a nice picture on the package of Hamburger Helper. The real beef is what we do *after* we set it.

Contemporaries credited Mahatma Gandhi with "single-handedly bringing down the British Empire" and giving India its independence. Remarkably, he achieved this goal in his lifetime by non-violent means, in strict accordance with his moral code. Is there anything we can learn from him?

For one, he didn't seem like a man plagued by self-doubt. His resolve was legendary. But there was something else. He was able to instantly change his way of life to follow his convictions. He gave up his Western-style clothes in favor of a homespun loincloth, traveled India in third class, lived among the poor, went to jail, and fasted for months on end. He clearly put every part of his daily existence in service of his goal.

Do our choices day-by-day, hour-by-hour, and minute-by-minute support our goals? When they do, we get ahead. When they don't, we suffer a setback. It's a simple rule with no exceptions. We all get it. So what's the problem?

The problem appears to be rooted in our own brains. In the immortal words of Pogo the Possum, *"We have met the enemy and he is us."* In addition to our logical goal-oriented brain, we have an emotional instant-gratification-procrastination-oriented counterbrain. The counterbrain is made up of habits, temptations, excuses, distractions, and other counterproductive behaviors. It is responsible for junk food cravings, hitting the snooze button, the rejection of all things new and different, and most things that you think in your head, but don't say out loud.

If you work with other people, you come into frequent contact with their counterbrains. Counterbrains cause problems. This is just a small sample of the types of problems you can expect from heightened counterbrain activity in the workplace:

Job Title	Biggest Challenge at Work
Sr. VP of E-Learning Services	*"Keeping employees focused"*
Call Center Director	*"Call center employee engagement"*
General Manager	*"Sales motivation"*
Managing Director	*"Driving a performance culture"*
COO	*"Productivity and motivation"*

What can you do?

Counterbrain works the same whether you are trying to manage other people or just yourself. Taking it head-on is unwise, because it knows you better than you know it. It has already obliterated hundreds of your good intentions and cannot wait to chew up one more.

If you really want to reach your goals and work effectively through other people, your best bet is to have the collective counterbrain on your side. This means *use the inert and addictive parts of the brain to visually and emotionally connect to your goal.* Bring the goal into your workspace and your daily routine. Then do the same for your employees.

An easy example of this is keeping score. As a teen, I was good at basketball. Our high school gym teacher noticed me right away. But instead of praising my natural gifts, he bullied me in front of the whole class. One time he said, "Eisenhauer, you think you are hot shit, but I don't see a championship banner on the gym wall with your name on it. Until you hang one there, you might as well go hide in the corner with your tail between your legs."

I don't know if he was a kick-ass coach who knew how to bring out the warrior spirit in boys—or a sadistic asshole—but his words struck a chord. From that day forward, my goal became to prove him wrong. In two years, I made the all-state team for basketball and soccer. I led my teams to win countless league and district titles. I played with and against future NBA greats, Kobe Bryant, Rip Hamilton, Donyell Marshall, and pros from the New Jersey Nets.

Besides sticking it to my teacher, it was *the game* itself that pulled me in. If I just got paid for shooting baskets, I'd feel dumb and be bored, and I'd miss a lot more shots. But because there was a game going on, people were shouting, and I could see the score. I'd shift into high gear and feel awesome. In hindsight, it's no coincidence that I ended up in the business of engaging people in their work. Once you are infected with the thrill of the game, you never settle for anything less.

GIVE REAL-TIME FEEDBACK

My first job after high school was waiting tables. It was another fast-paced game. The restaurant got so busy at night, it seemed like complete chaos. But if you kept up with it, you could walk out with $400 in your pocket—tips are a great way to keep score! There were no fans to cheer me on and no coach to call the plays. Instead, I was one-on-one, face-to-face with the customers. And there was no mistaking a pissed-off customer for a happy one. The feedback was clear and immediate. I learned from it and changed course daily. (Kind of like A/B testing for you marketing folks.)

Later, I worked at a knitting factory, a Coke bottling plant, a few retail stores, offices … It didn't matter where I worked, one thing was clear. Whenever I was removed from the results of my work and the immediate impact of my actions, performance became a concept. Motivation became a buzzword. Nothing changed. Nobody cared. I no longer felt *in the game*. And yet, there *was* a game going on in all of those places. What business isn't about scoring? It was my work environment that made me deaf and blind to it.

GET IN THE GAME

These days, companies are waking up to the necessity of bringing everyone, not just the top brass, into the game. Software companies are making big money outfitting sales and customer service teams with videogame-like dashboards. They call it "gamification."

> *Gamification motivates people with data on goals met, transparency about everyone's progress and collaboration, instant feedback, while giving employees a sense of community.*[9]

Basically, when you do what the company wants you to do, you get points. You can get points for anything: taking calls, making sales, completing tasks, staying within time limits. If your company wants you to collaborate and share your work, you get points for asking and answering questions, commenting, blogging, and uploading files for public use. If your company wants you to compete against your colleagues, it puts everyone else's scores on your dashboard. You can see the points add up instantly, just like when you are playing a videogame. Now you've got something else to watch, besides the clock.

Does it work?

In 2013, *Fast Company* published a case study on LiveOps, an outsourced virtual call center. LiveOps hires independent contractors and sells them as "brand ambassadors" to clients like eBay and AAA. Meanwhile, not only do these people dial for dollars and read from a script all day, they do it from their homes. All 20,000 of them.

That's a tough crowd to get to stick around their own company, let alone advocate for somebody else. LiveOps hired Bunchball, Inc. to set up a gamification platform for its call agents. It looked like this:

> … *Agents could get badges and points if they completed additional training and certifications.*
>
> … *They received reward points for increased call conversion, and all points were tracked on public leader boards.*
>
> … *Sharing knowledge, coaching, and networking were also rewarded with badges and real-time feedback.*

Bunchball reported that *"within a week of launching the program, 80% of LiveOps agents opted in and three-quarters of them return on a bi-weekly basis. Participating agents outperformed peers by 23% in average call-handle time and boosted customer satisfaction by 9%."*[10]

If gamification sounds like a trick, it's because it is. It won't solve major workplace problems we've discussed earlier, like the lack of intrinsic motivation, employees poorly matched to jobs, or confusion about the larger business context. However, with bigger concerns out of the way, there's nothing wrong with using a mind trick to get people to focus on the task at hand.

After all, our minds trick us all the time. Why not beat them at their own game?

Sometimes it's the stupidest things that get you excited. Our big game at Axero used to be making sales. One day I put a customer's logo on our webpage. Then another. Then another. We became obsessed with filling up the whole page with customer logos. Every time we added one, it gave all of us a boost.

Now the game is marketing. How do we let people know about us? How do we get them to come to the website? Premium content, baby! Free searchable, downloadable eBooks. I have an app on my phone that keeps track of all downloads. It's the first thing I check when I get up in the morning. I used to swipe every single alert to see who was downloading our eBooks and why. Now I just check the stats throughout the day. Twenty-five downloads in the past fifteen minutes. It makes me want to write more!

NEVER MIND SETBACKS

No matter what you do to rivet yourself to your goal, sometimes you will lapse. If you are in the habit of procrastinating, you will put off important tasks. Mark Twain wrote, *"Habit is habit and not to be flung out of the window by any man, but coaxed downstairs a step at a time."* (Pudd'nhead Wilson's Calendar.) Your best weapon against an occasional setback is to plan for it. It will happen whether you like it or not. The difference is how much significance you attach to it. Failure is the biggest distraction of all. And that's really all it is.

My least favorite task is editing blog posts. Back in our days of relentless SEO, we hired a writer squad to crank them out. I was never short of ideas to pitch to the writers, and we ended up with hundreds of posts queued for release. Everything was going well until I sat down and read a few. Okay, so these were not exactly Shakespeare sonnets, but still damn good info with plenty to take away. They were just missing some finishing touches and—hell—I could fix that! Well, as soon as I opened one of these posts, I'd find a bulletproof excuse to shut it off.

One day I had an epiphany: I was never going to finish them, unless … I decided to put them live on the website as is. Now whenever I had to choose between editing blog posts and doing something more pleasant, like scrubbing my toilet, I'd choose the posts. Why? Because I knew that at that very moment someone was reading my blog.

FIND A BUDDY

Focusing on the right things is not easy for anyone, especially at work. If it were, we wouldn't have so many people making all kinds of money as business and life coaches. Imagine not only giving your phone number to a bothersome stranger—but actually paying him to use it. This is by no means an indictment of people who hire personal coaches. It just goes to show you that you can't always defeat the distractions by yourself. Sometimes you need a friend.

One thing coaches and coachees get right is that the best motivation comes from other people. Gadgets and apps are not the only way to keep focused. Their true purpose is to connect you to other people. To see what's going on in their lives and minds while you are busy getting through your day. To get why *you* matter. We are all here to make a difference for somebody. And we need to hear from that somebody and, even better, see the difference we've made with our own eyes.

The coach is training wheels, someone to hold you pseudo-accountable until you build a direct link to people who need and value your work. Ideally, you'd feel less accountable and more empowered in your own right to be *in the game* together. The more people you have like that in your world, the more focused and successful you are. Which is why we end our survey of the individual employee with a strong call to ... Network!

CHAPTER 6

NETWORK

> ❝ In the long history of humankind (and animal kind, too) those who learned to collaborate and improvise most effectively have prevailed. ❞
>
> — CHARLES DARWIN

> ❝ In the business world, an executive knows something about everything, a technician knows everything about something, and the switchboard operator knows everything. ❞
>
> — HAROLD COFFIN, American writer

In 2012 a group of network scientists conducted a case study at a large aerospace firm. The scientists wondered whether internal connections helped the engineers succeed at their jobs. They looked at two measures of success: filing patents and bringing new products to market. It turned out that the number and quality of connections were the second most important success factor, after a related variable, the length of employment.

Drake Baer of *Fast Company* reported the results in a January 17, 2013 article, *Harvard Professor Finds That Innovative Ideas Spread Like The Flu; Here's How To Catch Them*. The study found that successful individuals had strong relationships across departments and up and down the chain of command. Similarly, the most successful teams were also the most interwoven and connected to the rest of the company.

He explains that ideas, insights and inspiration spread from person to person, much like office gossip or the flu. Those in the center of large, densely populated networks are the first to get new information and gather input on projects—an advantage over those working in isolation. Well-networked teams exchange ideas with the entire organization, gain the broadest perspective and command the most support.

Two heads are better than one. Four heads are better than two, and so on. Even if you are a rocket scientist, you are still only one person. While you are working on an important piece of the puzzle, you may be missing out on ten others. And if people don't have full access to each other's knowledge, neither will their final product.

It's Axero's business to advocate for knowledge sharing and collaboration. But we are not the only ones sounding the alarm. All kinds of companies are making it their top priority to get people to think and work together—like these managers who took our survey:

Job Title	Biggest Challenge at Work
Ops Manager	*"Collaboration"*
Product Manager	*"Collaboration on a global scale"*
Team Manager	*"Teams that are siloed"*
Engineering Manager	*"Keeping consultants feeling engaged with the company"*

Notice that the Harvard study doesn't mention *the quality of people* in your network, only *the strength of your connection* to them. That means bad people can help you, too, and excluding them from your network can hurt your chances for success.

This is probably the least intuitive piece of advice in this chapter, so let's dwell on it for a moment. We generally don't mind working with other people, as long as they think and work like we do, treat us well and play fair. Up to a point, these are all reasonable demands, and any company with a strong collaborative spirit should strive to satisfy them. Precisely how to go about it is the subject of the entire Part Three of this book, *Empower the Culture.*

That being said, sometimes we don't have the luxury of surrounding ourselves with like-minded and trustworthy individuals. And sometimes, we just don't know how to shut up and listen. So the real problem is us. In both cases, we are in danger of losing our focus, missing opportunities, and, in general, letting our ego call the shots.

Silencing your inner judge can be your best networking strategy. But you don't need to blindly trust people, either. Ask what's in it for them and learn to listen for their motives. I have also learned that to get to people's knowledge and skills, you have to go through their egos. Most of the time it's worth it.

Your company and your people are better off working together more often in more different ways. The question is: how do you get them to? Any ideas? Reward collaboration? Maybe. Social intranet? Of course. But before we talk policy or technology, let's rule out the obvious.

MAKE THE INTRODUCTIONS

New hires are not the only ones who need to be introduced. Unless you work for a really small company, there are people in your company and in your office who don't know each other. This is not something to be fixed overnight, but you can start by taking every opportunity to connect your people. Every time you have a meeting, make sure everyone knows everyone else. Especially in virtual meetings. Don't limit yourself to formal introductions. You already know that most people will snooze through those. Say something interesting and personal about each person you introduce, and—if they are not wallflowers—let them speak for themselves.

Make it a point that your people walk out of every corporate event knowing more coworkers than they did when they walked in. Ask managers and long-term employees to make introductions. Play those goofy networking games. Who doesn't like to discover something in common with another human being? It doesn't matter if they hate the same TV show or binge on the same ice cream flavor—people bond over the dumbest things. If some people shy away from fellow humans, it's only because they feel uninteresting or unwelcome. Or maybe they over-focus on differences, controversies and downsides. These are the same reasons that keep people from sharing knowledge and contributing fully in the workplace. Help them get over it!

BLOW THEIR HORN

The easiest way to get people to take interest in one another is to praise them.

Who is the first person others to go to with questions, problems, and ideas? Right. The boss. If the boss doesn't have the answer, he should know who would. Makes sense. But what if everyone in the company knew who the experts were? Not just the incomparable geniuses, but everyone on the team. What if people really understood and appreciated what everyone else does for the company?

For one, it would make running the company a lot easier. The other day, Nick, our sales guy, asked me for a .pdf file with all the product features. I called Trevor, our graphic designer and put the two of them together. Nick understands the customer better than I do. Trevor understands our product and visual arts. Once they know about each other, they can do this without me. Next time, I won't even have to call the meeting.

When introducing team members, take a moment to mention a few things that impress you about each one. Let them know that you hire people who are better and smarter than you. I like to say that we have an open door policy. Virtually speaking. Anyone can always come to me with any question. But if it's a question about sales, I would have to ask Nick anyway, so why not go to him first?

Make sure that credit for each project goes to the right people. If you are the formal lead, but someone else did 99 percent of the work, broadcast it to your people, so they know whom to see to get things done.

BE INCLUSIVE

The Internet's famous 1% Rule states that only 1 percent of users of any given internet community actively create content. Nine percent comment on other people's posts, and the remaining 90 percent are lurkers or silent consumers. For work sites, the ratio is different, but the fact remains: instead of openly contributing their knowledge and ideas, many people hang back and let others do the talking.

Lurking on Facebook is okay. But lurking at work robs the individual and the company of his full potential. And yet, many companies are unwittingly encouraging lurking by the way they communicate. Anytime you let important messages trickle down the chain of command, use one-way media like faxes and email blasts, or exclude certain people altogether, you train your employees to be passive. In Part Three, *Empower the Culture,* we will look closely at how companies talk to employees (Chapter 18, *Communicate*), how employees talk to companies (Chapter 19, *Give Them a Voice*), and how everyone can weigh in and participate fully (Chapter 20, *Default to Open*). For now, let's take one simple case.

Here's a company that gets it. It happens to be a chain of pawnshops in the Bay Area. But it could be any company anywhere. They are part of a trend that is massive, global and irreversible. Listen to Rebecca Verhoeff, Executive Vice President of Best Collateral, and see if you agree:

> *In the past, we relied on managers and faxes in a trickle-down approach to communication. Managers would send what we call "Daily Rah Rahs," which are reports on daily sales and loan activity. But these reports were only circulated in email to the management team. Employees weren't getting the information consistently, so they couldn't celebrate successes, participate in discussions, or gain insights from business trends. The company's daily productivity results were faxed to all stores,*

then posted to bulletin boards. Communication was limited to what was on the fax. No one could say, "Hey! Good job!" Or, "Hey, we need to do this differently." These were one-way, impersonal dispatches. There was a gap between what we communicated to managers and what employees actually heard. We needed to bridge that gap with one repository—a single place where people could go and access relevant information to their roles.[11]

First thing the management did was to connect growth opportunities to more inclusive communication.

We knew if we could continue to facilitate better communications, we could continue to grow the business, serve customers, and attract and retain great employees.

A big, giant, enormous step for a small, low-key, low-tech company—which led to support at the top and more strategic thinking.

… Yes, we had some initial hesitations. What if someone says something inappropriate in chat? HR compliance is a huge issue for us. …We even considered turning chat off. But the reality is, we can't read every email employees create. If employees want to do something inappropriate, there are many less obvious ways for them to do so. This social platform is pretty open and visible. I think we've

*built the kind of culture where there would be a
negative reaction if anyone conducted themselves
in an inappropriate manner within this forum.*

The launch strategy was three parts carrot and one part stick. Entice employees with useful content and social networking. Order the managers to do their rah-rahs in the new system—but let them log in from phones and tablets.

*... One of our senior managers was pretty skeptical
at first. "One more system, one more thing to do."
He wasn't used to using social media to begin with.
But we started off using just the document management tools, so most employees got it right away.
When managers saw the results of the improved
communication and access to documents in one
central place, they started to get it, too.*

One year later, the company is transformed.

*We've gone so far beyond faxed copies on a bulletin
board ... Managers or employees post daily results
4–5 times a day. The President is posting and
making comments. People at all roles and levels
are posting daily achievements, from individual
sales to upsells to store tactics. Employees coach each
other—from a distance ... People are moderating
and policing themselves. It's like positive peer pressure ... People have been celebrating each other's
successes. Sometimes someone will comment, "Its*

been a slow day," and someone from 100 miles away might say, "Hey, chin up, you can do it!" People post pictures of their kids or when they get engaged. We haven't had one incident of anyone posting anything remotely unprofessional or inappropriate. In fact, we've gotten some really funny photos.

If you look closely you'll see that all of Best Collateral's impressive results point to one simple shift in employees' attitude: people are *happy* to do what's expected of them and more! Human-to-human connection actually solves the employee's dilemma we talked about in Chapter 1. As people's relationships to one another change, so does their relationship to work. It's no longer about trading happiness for money. It's about being there for somebody else.

MAKE IT EASY FOR EMPLOYEES TO NETWORK

Well-networked employees are happy employees. TINYpulse 2013 Employee Engagement Survey of 40,000 employees at more that 300 companies discovered that, *"employee happiness is more dependent on co-workers than direct managers"* and that *"team play and collaboration are the top trait employees love about their co-workers."*

That includes the bosses. A well-networked company takes a load off management. That's because people are so much more capable than we give them credit for. When we remove the bottlenecks—ourselves—the business takes care of itself and things spontaneously move in the right direction.

Did I tell you how we started Communifire? It wasn't a product at first. We created it so we could stay on top of projects, submit bugs, and give customers 24-hour support. In our early days, Axero was your typical software guild. We had developers in India, customers all over the world, and sales and service reps in all different time zones. We didn't see a good product out there that was easy on the budget and met our needs. So we wrote our own.

When it went live, we invited our customers to try it out. We had no idea what to expect, but the system proved itself early on. I'd get up in the morning and see an SOS message from a customer. I'd think, "Oh, shit," and then I'd see that someone else had already responded.

You'd think a networking tool would be a big distraction at work. Who's going to work if everyone's posting and commenting? As they say about old age, it's bad—until you consider the alternative. Have you ever been to a meeting? We found that real-time asynchronous communication accomplishes everything a meeting does in less time with less disruption. As proof, we didn't have any meetings for five years. Recently we started having them every now and then, because we grew nostalgic. We just wanted everyone to look at each other again and feel like, "Wow! We *are* a company!"

Change is hard. New software is annoying. People want to interact with people, not systems. Luckily, today's employees, young and old, come equipped with social media networking skills. Give them an intuitive piece of software and a reason to use it, and they won't disappoint. One last story before we wrap up.

HubSpot is an Internet marketing provider and one of *Boston Business Journal's* perennial favorites for "Best Places to Work in Massachusetts." The company has been so successful at networking with employees that it has moved multiple corporate functions to social platforms. For example:

Recruiting. All HubSpot employees can headhunt for the company through their own social networks by using Jobvite, a social recruiting tool that integrates with LinkedIn, Facebook, Twitter, and other online networks. HubSpot also uses Work With Us, Jobvite's Facebook app, to help employees spread the word about job openings.

Performance Management. In 2012, HubSpot decided to do away with the annual performance review in favor of real-time continuous social performance management. The company chose Work.com by Salesforce.com. Now anyone of 500+ employees can give feedback to any other employee anytime. Employees can also track progress towards goals online and share results.

We've come to the end of Part One, urging you to empower the individual employee. There are different ways of empowering people, from matching job duties to character traits—to letting them set goals and track daily progress. Yet, no matter how qualified and motivated your people are, they can accomplish nothing by themselves.

Companies exist so that people can build on each other's skills and knowledge. Even so, in the past only a few individuals at any company had a breadth of connections. The rest toiled in relative isolation. Web 2.0 leveled the playing field. Now the technology is there to give every employee in the company access to every fellow employee and to all the information being shared within the company. This access is the real power.

PART TWO
EMPOWER THE RELATIONSHIP

> ❝ If you need something from somebody always give that person a way to hand it to you. ❞
>
> — SUE MONK KIDD, *The Secret Life of Bees*

> ❝ So much of what we call management consists in making it difficult for people to work. ❞
>
> — PETER DRUCKER

> ❝ I believe the best managers acknowledge and make room for what they do not know—not just because humility is a virtue but because until one adopts that mindset, the most striking breakthroughs cannot occur. ❞
>
> — ED CATMULL, *Creativity, Inc.*

CHAPTER 7
A MANAGER'S VIEW: WHAT KIND OF BOSS ARE YOU?

" Nothing is more critical to your happiness than learning to manage your boss. The alternative can be a disaster. If your boss tries to turn the tables and manage you, the next thing you know, you'll be doing moronic tasks in return for money. "

— SCOTT ADAMS, *The Joy of Work*

" I've spent nearly forty years thinking about how to help smart, ambitious people work effectively with one another. The way I see it, my job as a manager is to create a fertile environment, keep it healthy, and watch for the things that undermine it. "

— ED CATMULL, Creativity, Inc.

In her quest for sound performance management, Shelly Carlin of Motorola Solutions stumbled onto the biggest roadblock to employee engagement: the toxic boss. She handled it strategically, by scrapping a system that turned managers into fearsome judges, and replacing it with one that trained them to be supportive coaches.

The new system focused on building relationships between managers and their direct reports. Whatever helped the relationship, like a personalized performance review, became the new norm. Anything that got in the way, like the ratings, went out the window.

Whether or not you agree with her methods, Shelly had the right idea. If you count on your managers to engage people, trust works better than fear. Just think back to your own career. If you

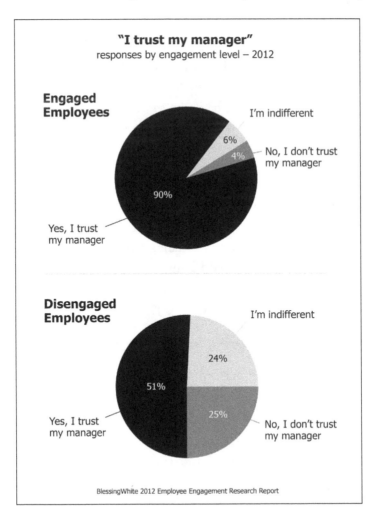

"I trust my manager"
responses by engagement level – 2012

Engaged Employees

I'm indifferent
6%
4%
No, I don't trust my manager
90%
Yes, I trust my manager

Disengaged Employees

I'm indifferent
24%
51%
25%
Yes, I trust my manager
No, I don't trust my manager

BlessingWhite 2012 Employee Engagement Research Report

are a *Dilbert* fan, that's the moral of the comic strip. Or, if you prefer research with your morning coffee, a lot of it points to the same conclusion. For example, a 2012 survey by BlessingWhite found a strong dependency between disengagement and erosion of trust in immediate supervisors.

If you believe this chart, there aren't a lot of reasonably engaged folks who mistrust their bosses. The reverse is not true, however, as plenty of people who trust their bosses loathe their jobs. Which corroborates a well-known fact that a boss has more ways of disempowering and disengaging you than just losing your trust. Let's look at some popular techniques:

> *The Indecisive Boss. Leaders are indecisive for a variety of reasons. Some may be perfectionists who won't make decisions until they gather all the data; others are paralyzed by uncertainty; and many simply prefer the seeming safety of the status quo ...*[12]

Recall Betsy from Chapter 1 and her struggle to move her project along. Indecisive bosses rob us of our sense of purpose and stand in the way of our success. Even a single failure to keep up the momentum, can turn a fireball employee into a paycheck-collecting robot. Imagine what you do to your people's will to succeed, when you get in their way as a matter of course.

> *The Insecure Manager. Managers are supposed to motivate employees, not compete with them. Yet, many supervisors inhibit talented employees and good ideas because of their own insecurities ...*

Cheating people out of their full potential shuts off another intrinsic motivator: mastery. Aside from the obvious consequences, guess who else on the team doesn't get to grow and move up? That's right, the boss. Did you wonder how my boss from Beauty Co. had kept himself at the same desk for twenty-odd years? Mystery solved!

> *The All-Knowing Leader. Some executives think they know it all. They assume they are the smartest people in the room, feel they are the only ones interested in succeeding, and constantly tell stories about how they pulled off impossible things in the past. They also believe that without them, everything will fall apart. Such leaders aren't incompetent, but you wish they would trust more, listen more, and be more inclusive …*

The self-important boss—although at times useful as a mentor and for delegating up—is a threat to our autonomy and, ultimately, a drain on employee engagement and development. If the above paragraph sounds anything like you, congratulations on building your track record. Now get over it and take notice of other people's talents and contributions. Besides, you can always pride yourself on how humble you are.

The more boss-managing advice you read, the more you realize what a hazard a manager is in the workplace. From stifling creativity and sitting on important decisions to outright driving valuable employees to the competition—any manager is a potential source of untold suffering and loss. You can try to mitigate the risk with training and selection, but none are 100 percent foolproof.

WHAT IF WE GOT RID OF MANAGERS ALTOGETHER?

Is it any wonder that the number one best company to work for in America, Google, has already asked and answered this question?

> *A few years into the company's life, founders Larry Page and Sergey Brin actually wondered whether Google needed any managers at all. In 2002 they experimented with a completely flat organization, eliminating engineering managers in an effort to break down barriers to rapid idea development and to replicate the collegial environment they'd enjoyed in graduate school.*[13]

After a couple of months, Larry and Sergey had to bring the managers back. The two of them simply couldn't answer all the questions, give all the feedback, and break up all the fights in the company. But even though the flat-Google experiment satisfied the founders, it failed to settle the issue for those bearing the brunt of management on their shoulders. Time after time, as Google's people analytics team sat down to decode another employee survey, they faced the same question: *"Do managers matter?"* In other words, are some managers better than others? If so, how can poor managers improve? And what should be the extent of a manager's call of duty?

As we've seen from their hiring practices, there is no shortage of original thinking at Google. And, when anyone at Google thinks he has an answer, there is a language he needs to speak: data. The people analytics team, counting several PhD statisticians in their ranks, went to work. To everyone's great relief, it turned out that management did, indeed, matter.

> *For example, in 2008, the high-scoring managers saw less turnover on their teams than the others did—and retention was related more strongly to manager quality than to seniority, performance, tenure, or promotions. The data also showed a tight connection between managers' quality and workers' happiness: Employees with high-scoring bosses consistently reported greater satisfaction in multiple areas, including innovation, work-life balance, and career development ...[14]*

By cross-referencing employee surveys and performance reviews, the statisticians figured out what the best managers did differently. The "8 key behaviors" became the definition of a front-line manager at Google and the focus of future management evaluation and training.

A good manager:
1. *Is a good coach*
2. *Empowers the team and does not micromanage*
3. *Expresses interest in and concern for team members' success and personal well-being*
4. *Is productive and results-oriented*
5. *Is a good communicator—listens and shares information*
6. *Helps with career development*

7. *Has a clear vision and strategy for the team*
8. *Has key technical skills that help him or her advise the team*[15]

Would you like to meet one of Google's best?

In 2011, Google made headlines when it paid one of its executives, Neal Mohan, $100 million to keep him from going to Twitter. Mohan was in charge of Google's display advertising product and strategy. Two years later, *Business Insider* interviewed Mohan's present and past direct reports to find out what it was like to work for him:

> *"He's not a screamer or a big table-banger."*
>
> *"You don't waste a lot of time in meetings with Neal, that's for sure."*
>
> *"If I escalate something to him, I know that he will return a response."*
>
> *"He gives you a lot of autonomy, but believes in defining big, specific, and strategic goals."*
>
> *"Every three months, he makes sure there is not a lot of redundancy in his product line, which is critical because in ad tech, everything has to sync."*
>
> *"He doesn't bullshit. If our numbers were going bad, I heard from him."*
>
> *"I never had to talk to him unless I needed to. It was awesome."*[16]

At the core of a great boss-employee relationship is the understanding that empowerment is not a zero-sum game. An employee's loss is not a manager's gain. Rather, the opposite is true. The best managers make things happen by empowering other people. Then tasks get accomplished effortlessly, and big ambitious projects move within reach.

When you squelch your people, the pattern is reversed. You create resistance in your team, then struggle to overcome it. Simple tasks become difficult, and great accomplishments become impossible. The more you try, the further you disconnect, the less you accomplish. It's a vicious cycle.

Of course, no manager means for this to happen. But managers are human, and they have blind spots. This part of the book spotlights where the relationship between an employee and his next in command can get off track. It's about minding individual relationships, not leading an entire organization—we will get to that in Part Three.

The next seven chapters are my take on the seven deadly sins of people management:

Don't	Do
Overwhelm them with boring tasks they hate	Use them or lose them
Make them feel like they are in a dead-end job	Support career development
Take credit for their work and self-aggrandize at their expense	Make them visible
Micromanage	Let go of your inner micromanager
Be fake and remote	Be authentic
Slave-drive	Help
Lose their loyalty and drive	Reward like a king

Great managers work hard to overcome their shortcomings. You may have battled some of these successfully. Yet, others are so ingrained they have become your second nature. The better we understand the hidden pitfalls of people management, the more we are able to resist their siren call.

CHAPTER 8
USE THEM OR LOSE THEM

" I swallowed a moon made of iron

They refer to it as a nail

I swallowed this industrial sewage, these unemployment
documents

Youth stooped at machines die before their time

I swallowed the hustle and the destitution

Swallowed pedestrian bridges, life covered in rust

I can't swallow any more

All that I've swallowed is now gushing out of my throat

Unfurling on the land of my ancestors

Into a disgraceful poem. "

— XU LIZHI [17]

The poem at the beginning of this chapter belongs to a dead Chinese boy. Xu Lizhi was only twenty-four when he jumped out of a window of his work dormitory in Southern China. Xu came from a small village to work the assembly line at Foxconn, a contract manufacturer of popular electronic gadgets. The reason for his suicide: monotony and harsh conditions of his job.

Escaping work drudgery can take many forms. From day-trading on company time all the way to jumping out of the company window. Neither is desirable from the employer perspective. As a preventive measure, the company might limit Internet access—or hang safety nets under the windows, as Foxconn has done. Such steps may discourage a specific behavior, but they won't win dedication and commitment. For that to happen, the job itself must appeal to the employee.

This might be too much to ask of Foxconn factories—or the slave-manned fishing boats off the coast of Thailand. Unfortunately, one doesn't need to be born into poverty or travel to exotic lands to feel drained and disgusted at work. Plenty of people right here in the U.S. would rather be doing something else during their regular business hours.

Like what?

Twenty-four percent of those surveyed by BlessingWhite in 2012 said *"more opportunities to do what I do best"* is key to their job satisfaction. The report also says that the main reason employees stay at their jobs is because they like the work they do.

I think a lot of people would be upset if I made Steve Jobs out to be a model people manager. However, it is a fact that he assembled an all-star team of professionals reporting directly to him. We know he didn't do it by stroking their egos or maintaining their work-life balances. Rather, what he had to offer was so powerful that it made up for his poisonous personality and superhuman demands. All this at a time when Apple wasn't even making the kind of money it does today.

> *Your work is going to fill a large part of your life,*
> *and the only way to be truly satisfied is to do what*
> *you believe is great work. And the only way to do*

great work is to love what you do. If you haven't found it yet, keep looking. Don't settle.[18]

That was Steve Jobs speaking to Stanford graduates in 2005. Ironically, Jobs' Apple did not create the kind of culture where every employee loved to come to work. Rather the opposite, especially if you include one of Apple's subcontractors, Foxconn. Nevertheless, it accomplished spectacular results by letting key people do exactly what they loved to do.

When was the last time you asked your people if they were thrilled with their jobs or just settling for a paycheck? Most of the time, not settling is not even on the menu. And yet, the best managers don't ask people to settle for less than doing great work they love. They understand what people like about their jobs. They provide work that absorbs people mentally, physically, and emotionally, and is challenging for the right reasons.

To do that, you'll need to learn people's personalities and skills. Be curious. Observe. What questions do they ask and answer? What turns them on? What makes them angry? Everyone loves to complain about work. So, it's easy to save your breath and just ignore the whining. But there's a flip side to the complaints:

WHAT WOULD THEY RATHER DO?

I'm not suggesting you walk around the office all day asking every employee this question. (Although, on second thought, it might not be such a bad idea!) As you know, my company doesn't even have an office. But we do have something that allows us to be many places at once: a social intranet. Most of the time, our managers don't even need to ask. Shared workspace makes it easy for people to volunteer on projects that interest them and weigh in on topics they care about. And it helps the managers, too, because it lets us see how people work. Two quick stories about that.

Bryce handles our customer service. He knows the product cold and makes the customer feel like a king. Clearly, a good fit all around. On the other hand, he is not necessarily the visual or graphical type, so it wouldn't have occurred to me to ask him to design user interfaces. Except that it has occurred to Bryce. Bryce went ahead and created a mock-up for a new feature a customer had asked for. That's how I found out where he drew the line between what he did for the customer and what he handed off to the team.

Even though Bryce's mock-up didn't look anything like the finished product, it saved us a ton of time. He had clearly thought through the details and came up with the right solution. All we had to do was to make sure a three-year old could use it. Now, when a customer asks for a custom feature, Bryce gives us the starting point. The designers and developers take it from there. It takes him away from the customers, but the trade-off is worth it. It makes his entire job cycle more fulfilling—and the work he does is excellent.

Another trick to rediscovering your people and their hidden talents is "white space." Many people find their most productive and creative moments during unplanned and unscheduled activities. LinkedIn cancels all meetings a few days each month, so that employees can work on something they are passionate about. It's called "hack days," and it's standard practice with many tech firms.

Vivek and I have been back and forth on hack days or hack half-days or some hack hours here and there. In the end we decided it was a luxury Axero could not afford right now. However, the idea had stuck with us, and eventually came to life in a way that fit our picture.

Our lead software architect, Raghav, started as a programmer in our India office. We knew from the beginning that he was pretty good. So when we needed a JavaScript expert on the team, we asked Raghav if he thought he could learn it. He said yes. We said, great, we'll check back with you in a month. Raghav came back the next day and told us he had learned it. That's when we started asking him to do things we thought were impossible. But he would still come back the next day with a solution.

We were running out of big, important problems for Raghav to solve. We could easily fill his day with mundane tasks, but we were afraid he'd find a better use for his talents. *Use him or lose him.* That's when it hit us. We went to Raghav and said, "We are not going to tell you what to do anymore. You get our strategy. Go ahead and make any changes to the software that make sense to you. If you feel it will improve the product and help the customers, just do it. You don't need to ask our permission."

From that day forward, Communifire really took off. It became usable, interactive, cutting edge. He made hundreds of small changes, saving a click here, two clicks there. The end result: once a customer got on Communifire, they'd never leave.

LEAVE ROOM FOR GREAT IDEAS

Hack privileges are not just for tech stars. Any company can benefit from giving any employee creative freedom in his area of expertise. Just think of what happens when you don't. People come up with all kinds of ideas for product and process improvement all the time. It's natural, given how much time they spend doing the same tasks over and over again. However—and this is where smart management wins big—unless we are allowed to focus on our ideas, they seem less real than our daily to-do lists. That is until we see a competitor who has acted on the same idea. Then we add it to our list and play catch-up where we could have come out ahead.

It's a paradox: if we over-focus on the to-dos, we fall behind. If we had kept Raghav's nose to the grindstone, one of the two things would have happened. Either he would have left us, and our software would have fallen behind the competition's—or our software would have fallen behind, and he would have left us.

That, by the way, is exactly what happened to my younger brother Trevor and his former employer. Trev's been doing graphic design ever since high school. After college, he went to work for a local ad agency and quickly became their brightest star. He thrived on creative projects for big-budget clients, like Verizon and AT&T. Unfortunately, those were few and far between. Most of the work came from local restaurants who wanted tried-and-true and, most of all, cheap. On a good day, Trev would be resizing a picture of a steak and a wine glass. Other days, he would be cramming words into an ad space with no pictures at all.

It's easy to feel trapped in a job that takes away your self-esteem, especially when you are married with two kids and job security is a must. However, after two years of this, my brother was completely fed up with shitwork coming across his desk. He quit and came to work for me. I honestly don't know what happened to the ad agency and whether they still have those big-name clients. But, if I know anything about keeping customers, it's that you need to learn how to keep your best employees first.

LET THEM WIN

To keep good people, you need to know what motivates them. Remember Daniel Pink and his theory of human motivation? Autonomy is number one. Nothing motivates like being in charge. Whenever possible, let your people call the shots. Let them work on their ideas and see the fruit of their labors. Listen to the Starbucks CEO Howard Schultz:

> *To stay vigorous, a company needs to provide a stimulating and challenging environment for all these types: the dreamer, the entrepreneur, the professional manager, and the leader. If it doesn't, it risks becoming yet another mediocre corporation.*[19]

One of Starbucks' most successful moves was simply to allow a group of employees to act on their idea for a new drink. Howard Schultz tells the story in his 1999 memoir *Pour Your Heart Into It.* Here's the short version.

In 1993 a Santa Monica district manager, Dina Campion, suggested that Starbucks add a sweetened blended iced coffee drink to its menu. Schultz, a coffee purist, was horrified at the idea. However, another executive gave it the green light. A local store team perfected the recipe, and in the fall of 1994 the Starbucks Frappuccino was born. (Starbucks took the name of a discontinued product from Coffee Connection, a chain it acquired in 1994.) In its first full year on the national market, Frappuccino grossed $52 million. *Business Week* named it one of the best products of the year. Howard Schultz called it *"the best mistake I never made."*

Just like a doctor, a manager's first call of duty should be to "do no harm." Don't suck the joy out of people's work. Don't stand in the way of their productivity, creativity, and drive. Don't waste their talents. Let them contribute fully. Of course, none of this is easy. If you can keep the ball rolling and give people their space, you are far ahead of most managers. And yet, there is so much more you could do.

How about taking your people places they could never get without your guidance and support?

CHAPTER 9
SUPPORT CAREER DEVELOPMENT

❝ When you become a leader, success is all about growing others. ❞

— JACK WELCH

❝ Engineers hate being micromanaged on the technical side, but they love being closely managed on the career side. ❞

— ERIC CLAYBERG, Software-Engineering Manager, Google

My dad got me my first paying job when I was twelve. A local motorcycle dealer hired me to do whatever chores he deemed age-appropriate. One day I was sweeping the parking lot. It was windy, and the wind was blowing the dirt all over the pavement as fast as I was sweeping it. I couldn't be more miserable. After a while, the owner came out and gave me a patronizing smirk. "Tim," he said, "as long as you can sweep, you will always have a job."

The sarcasm of his words was lost on me at the time. Only years and countless dead-end jobs later did I grasp their true meaning. *There will always be shit jobs, Tim; and, as long as you are up for one, you can have it for the asking.* Who knows, maybe he really thought it was something a twelve-year-old wanted to hear.

Time proved him right. No matter how old I got or how many credentials—real or fictitious—I crammed into my résumé, shit jobs dominated my workscape. Everyone around me seemed to be paying their dues into a system that only rewarded them with more of the same. I decided that, if I was going to work my ass off, I might as well have some say in where I was headed. Then I joined a few startups. Then I met Vivek. Then we started Axero. And then, for the foreseeable future, the career path problem was solved.

Of course, starting your own company doesn't eliminate shitwork. It simply glorifies it. Shitwork is unavoidable. No matter how badly you want yourself and everyone else to hone your best skills, there will always be stuff that just needs to get done. How do you stay motivated when the work is not exactly its own reward? Look for the context of what you're doing. Am I a gofer or a boss-in-the-making? Do I see a bright future or a gigantic shit pile and a ticking clock?

People want a better tomorrow. And, if they are focused on their jobs, that means something to look forward to careerwise. A 2013 *Trends in Global Employee Engagement* report by Aon Hewitt cites *career opportunities* as the no. 1 driver of employee engagement in North America. BlessingWhite reports that 24 percent of employees rank *career development and training* as the most important factor in job satisfaction. Likewise, *poor career prospects* is the top reason for leaving. (BlessingWhite *Employee Engagement Research Update*, January 2013.)

Of all the tricks in this part of the book, career support is the most magical. Can you put a new and exciting spin on people's future? The late Steve Jobs was a master of the genre—another reason he could hire and keep great people despite being a boss from hell. A popular legend says he convinced CEO John Sculley to leave the highly successful Pepsi for the struggling Apple with an off-the-cuff, *"Do you want to sell sugared water for the rest of your life? Or do you want to come with me and change the world?"*

Don't wait for the annual evaluation to check in with your people. Sit down and talk to them as often as necessary. Understand and support their ambitions. Take advantage of the formal review to relieve their anxiety about the future.

What if you have a bitter pill up your sleeve? Tempting as it is to put off tough conversations, it doesn't work. Surprise criticism can breed resentment and drive a wedge between the manager and the employee. Instead, give real-time feedback throughout the year and use the review season to zero in on the future.

That said, everyone wants to hear that they have a bright future with the company they work for. But what if there is simply no room for promotion? This is Google's problem, according to Eric Clayberg, a front-line manager at Google. Eric became a manager after Google bought his company. However, for the rest of his team, climbing the ladder will not be so easy.

> *I was worried about the flat organizational structure at Google; I knew it would be hard to help people on my team get promoted. I learned in the classes about how to provide career development beyond promotions. I now spend a third to half my time looking for ways to help my team members grow.*[20]

There, you heard it. Career is not always about rapid promotion. Invest your time and skills in developing your people for the long run. Encourage breadth and depth of experience. Explain how current responsibilities will lead to future opportunities. Will they? Point out the skills they need to master and set aside the time and resources for that purpose. Build trust by honoring your commitments.

Helping people succeed is motivating and rewarding on both sides. Besides, it's much easier to boss people when you give them coaching and support in return. If you don't have their backs on their career paths, will they have yours on critical projects?

So, why wouldn't a manager give priority to developing his people? The rest of this chapter—and the whole of Part Two—assumes that you would. But, before we go on, let's play the devil's advocate.

"I DON'T HAVE TIME"

Of course not. But, if it isn't your people, then who and what has your time? Are the emails as urgent as they seem? Are the interruptions worth your while? Make time, insists McGill University professor Henry Mintzberg:

> *Slow down. Take a deep breath. Pause. Reflect. Coach ourselves; I think coaching ourselves is an interesting example of pausing and reflecting. Get together with a bunch of other managers for lunch to talk about the things important to us as managers.*[21]

Why does a Google manager have one-third to one-half of his workweek to invest in his team, and other managers don't have any time at all? It could be that they don't know how important it is—or they don't know how to unplug from the inbox. More likely, though, no one's asked them to, let alone trained them to be good at it. In that case, why not ask your boss for time and resources to develop your people? Make it a goal, agree on the details, and put it in your performance plan. What if your boss is not supportive? Go ahead and give him this book. I put a lot of thought into the title to make it easy for people to do just that.

"I'LL BE GONE IN A COUPLE OF YEARS, ANYWAY"

Some people blame management rotation programs for this mindset. Others blame general instability and turnover. In all fairness, you never know how long you will stay at a job. Besides, does it really matter? Your people skills, reputation, and relationships will follow you everywhere. If it's the staff turnover that makes you skeptical, can your coaching make a difference?

"IF I TELL THEM SOMETHING THEY DON'T WANT TO HEAR, THEY'LL GET DEFENSIVE"

Build trust. If you follow the principles in Part Two, it should be easy for you to have an open and honest discussion with any of your people. Set an example. Ask for their feedback and show them that you can handle anything they've got to say. Then turn the tables.

"I AM INSECURE AS A MANAGER AND JEALOUS OF MY STAFF"

Okay, no one actually says that. So, let me rephrase: *if you know someone who might feel threatened by a subordinate*, read to him this passage from *Insights for the Journey* by John Lucht:

If the business unit you are responsible for can turn in an outstanding performance and if the reason for that performance is that you have found truly excellent people, placed them in positions where their stellar talents will be best used, and empowered and encouraged them to do their best work, your superiors—and if not they, then outside recruiters—will be eager to apply your leadership to an even bigger business unit or perhaps the entire company.

Lucht goes on to remind us that by holding our people back, we stall our own careers. Ask yourself: am I more likely to get promoted if there is no one to fill my spot? Or if there is a capable, well-trained candidate right on my team?

There are many time-honored techniques for supporting and promoting your people, if that's what you want to do. Find one that suits your business and fits your personal style.

BE A MENTOR

Mentoring is as old as life itself. Animals mentor their young to help them survive in the wild. So much more do the junior associates need a guiding hand in the office jungle. I am speaking from personal experience, of course. Before Axero, I was a job hopper. If I lasted longer than a year at any job, it was because I had a mentor.

I've said a lot of nasty things about my job at Beauty Co.— and am not even halfway through my list. So, it's fair to ask, if it was so bad, how come I stayed there for two years? Well, I did have someone who took me under his wing and made my problems seem small and my tasks doable, even pleasant.

"Dan" was a manager who frequently gave me assignments, although he was not my direct boss. IT was Dan's second career. He still remembered what it was like to be a novice and understood the magic of well-timed advice. I didn't just go to him for help. I shadowed him on the job and had lunch with him all the time. The most important career lesson he taught me was how to deal with people.

Remember how intimidated I was by everyone at Beauty Co. when I first showed up? Dan noticed that I dreaded being left one-on-one with my technophobic coworkers, and gave me life-saving tips: No walking into HR unannounced and trying to fix their computers. Call ahead and schedule. Sales Department—totally different. Walk in anytime, as long as you are carrying food. Cookies for inside sales. Doughnuts for the outside reps. These were the magic pills that turned suspicious strangers into best friends. "Come on in, Tim! These damn computers! I'll just sit at this other one." He gave me the confidence to take problems head on, instead of retreating into myself.

Many companies have caught on to the virtues of mentorship. Instead of leaving it up to chance, they are purposefully matching employees with influential mentors. Take the world-famous M.D. Anderson Cancer Center at the University of Texas (no. 5 on Glassdoor's "Employees' Choice 50 Best Places to Work" in 2013). At Anderson, senior execs serve as mentors to all ranks of employees, not just the immediate reports. A mentor guides the employee along the career path, giving advice, selecting projects, and tracking progress towards goals. Employees can choose a mentor for a specific career track. Sometimes even more than one. For example, the Hospital

Administrative Fellowship Program allows participants full access to the entire senior operations team.

KEEP EVERYONE LEARNING

Not everything can be learned on the job. There is much technical knowledge and inspiration outside of the daily to-do. Many tech companies, like LinkedIn and Spotify, use their hack time to give and get tech talks or go to an outside event. If you've never sent an employee off to discretionary training, doing so could be scary. Are you opening yourself up to all kinds of requests?

Learn your team's goals, weaknesses and strengths. Help them find common ground between their interests and the company's. Choose courses that build on what they know. Encourage them to learn from one another.

TRANSPARENCY=LEARNING

If you want people to pay attention and learn fast, the best way is to let them see what's going on inside the company. With a small company like Axero, it's pretty easy. For example, we let everyone listen in on customer interviews. That means everyone gets to learn why different customers hire us and how they use our software.

We are very transparent about how we make decisions and run the company. Everyone has access to the same data. We've always been this way, since Vivek and I were a two-man show. It's more complicated for larger companies, but many are finding that the benefits outweigh the costs.

If you manage other people, it's your job to make sure they look forward to their professional future. Executive recruiter John Lucht writes in *Insights for the Journey* that a certain GE executive went as far as recommending his own best people for outside jobs. Lucht further reports that many of these individuals went to the interviews and got offers, but none ever left GE. *"In the end,"* he concludes, *"they couldn't leave a boss—and because of him a company—that so obviously respected them and cared about their professional development."*

CHAPTER 10
MAKE THEM VISIBLE

❝ I start with the premise that the function of leadership is to produce more leaders, not more followers. ❞
— RALPH NADER

❝ It is better to lead from behind and to put others in front, especially when you celebrate victory when nice things occur. You take the front line when there is danger. Then people will appreciate your leadership. ❞
— NELSON MANDELA

Theory without practice is dead. Coaching and guiding alone will not make a difference in anyone's career. If you really want to grow your people into experts and leaders, you must let them demonstrate their knowledge and lead.

Managers often act as gatekeepers to high-profile projects, important clients, and the higher-ups. Responsibility for other people's work comes with a temptation to hog the spotlight and pinch the credit. Resist it—if not for your people's sake, then for your own. If you're a boss that allows employees to shine, then good people will be eager to work for you. And that will make it easy for you to pick the best for your team.

Being in the spotlight is one of the most energizing experiences the workplace has to offer. Sure, sometimes we fall asleep in the stands. But who can remain sluggish and apathetic on the court, when the game is on and all the eyes are on you? The Institute for Corporate Productivity (i4cp) recommends that managers offer high-visibility and strategic assignments to engage their teams. For example: to research and present alternatives for a new idea, to participate in a cross-departmental project, or to attend an industry event and share it with the group.

These are all good ideas, but what if ...

"WHAT IF THERE ARE FEW OPPORTUNITIES FOR RANK-AND-FILE TO GET IN FRONT OF THE UPPER MANAGEMENT?"

You could create more.

LinkedIn lets employees pitch product ideas directly to top executives, including founder Reid Hoffman and CEO Jeff Weiner. The execs convene once a quarter to select projects for the LinkedIn idea incubator, called *[in]cubator*. Any employee can present any idea, as long as it benefits either customers or employees. The winning team gets an executive mentor and up to three months to work exclusively on the project. The company has approved five out of the first fifty submissions. One example is *go/book*, a meeting-booking tool for employees.

"WHAT IF NOBODY WANTS TO PARTICIPATE?"

You never know who in the company feels invisible until you give them a chance to speak up. Hell, it could even be the CEO!

One day a customer called us and said he wanted to talk CEO to CEO. I said, "Okay, I guess that would be me."

CUSTOMER: I run a moving company in
Massachusetts. I noticed that your background is
very similar to mine.
TIM: Oh, really?
CUSTOMER: Yes. Since I was a kid ...

I sat back and listened. His story clearly meant a lot to
him, and he really got into it. I even heard him clap his hands
in the background. After twenty-five minutes, he realized he
had been talking to himself about himself the entire time. He
abruptly thanked me for listening and hung up. I didn't even
get a chance to say goodbye.

Was he embarrassed by his unsolicited outpour? Maybe.
But he didn't need to be. Sharing is very rewarding. Every now
and again, we all need to turn our hearts inside out and let other
people see what's there. Of course, your timing and your audience
are important. But don't worry; there are an infinite number of
ways to arrange both. Here's how one company does it.

URX is a San Francisco-based startup riding the high tide of
digital ad technologies. TechCrunch first profiled URX in October
of 2013, after the company raised $3.1 million in round A. In April
of 2014, *The Wall Street Journal* published an article announcing
a $12 million deal for the startup, now valued at $40 million.

URX is busy spending all that money and proving its worth
to investors. However, CEO John Milinovich says they find time
for "learning for knowledge's sake." And they do it through
employee-featuring show-and-tell.

Several times a week, usually over lunch, the entire
team is invited to what they call Tech Talks. These

are always taught by another member of the team,
and can be about something related to a project
they are working on, a demo, or simply a relevant
topic they find interesting.

If you've done a good job matching people to jobs, expect them to jump at the chance to explain what it is that they do.

One of the more inspiring facets of this tactic is
seeing the people you work with double as teachers.
Many are willing to put the time into preparing
materials to discuss, and are very patient when
describing topics they know like the back of their
hand to people who are less familiar. For people
who work in a very specific functional area, the
ability to present, teach and mentor gives them an
extra set of tools they can apply in their careers,
either at URX or down the line.[22]

"WHAT IF AN EMPLOYEE DOESN'T WANT VISIBILITY?"

Right. Some people would rather be left in peace and leave the spotlight to others. My brother is one. He likes doing his job, not talking about it. In these cases, it's even more up to the manager to praise the unsung. Give credit generously. Defer to their judgment more often. Connect them directly to people who benefit from their work.

Quiet doesn't always mean content. Make sure you understand the ambitions of the genius in the back of the room.

What does he want? Is it more imaginative projects? New tools? Education? Money? Time off? If you don't know, ask!

"WHAT IF AN EMPLOYEE IS ALREADY WELL-KNOWN IN THE COMPANY?"

The world is bigger than the company. Give your people a chance to shine in front of the clients and peers everywhere.

Remember Raghav, our superstar lead programmer? We hired Raghav because he was a Microsoft MVP (Most Valuable Professional). Microsoft awards this title once a year to developers who are most active in the online communities. This is how we knew Raghav liked to write about ASP.NET and help other developers.

We built a website for Raghav and encouraged him to share his knowledge. We also gave him the freedom to code what he wanted. Whenever he crossed into an uncharted territory, he would write about it on his site. Today, Codeasp.net gets 100,000 visitors a month, and Raghav is one of the best-known ASP.NET developers in the world.

As the saying goes, everyone in the company has the same job: to make his boss look good. Don't be a scrooge and return the favor!

CHAPTER 11

LET GO OF YOUR INNER MICROMANAGER

❝ When I give a minister an order, I leave it to him to find the means to carry it out. ❞

— NAPOLEON BONAPARTE

❝ I believe that managers must loosen the controls, not tighten them. They must accept risk; they must trust the people they work with and strive to clear the path for them; and always, they must pay attention to and engage with anything that creates fear. ❞

— ED CATMULL, Creativity, Inc.

Remember how I built my first intranet working late nights without being paid? If you are thinking I was a mega-geek, you are essentially right. But there was another reason I took work home. My boss.

Il Duce, the help-desk micromanager, was not just a minor annoyance. He had an elaborate, ironclad system for breaking our concentration and disrupting our work. He could usually accomplish it in three steps:

STEP 1: Creep up behind a busy employee and start giving pointers and suggestions.

STEP 2: When out of pointers, ask the employee to show what he is working on. (Note: do not change the order of Step 1 and Step 2, otherwise your pointers may accidentally help the employee, thereby greatly diminishing the annoyance factor.)

STEP 3: When there is no more work to talk about, change the subject to showcase your knowledge of history or another equally irrelevant topic.

I don't know if there were any more steps up Il Duce's sleeve, because nobody on the IT team ever made it past the first three. We'd give up trying to get anything done and just sit there and hate our jobs.

Needless handholding kills trust, drains motivation, and sucks all the joy out of work. It's not just the employee who suffers. Chronic micromanagement overwhelms the boss and keeps him away from the things that truly need his attention. We all know it, but the tricky part is that nobody does it on purpose. We either can't help it or don't realize we are doing it at all.

IS IT POSSIBLE THAT YOU ARE A MICROMANAGER?

When in doubt, ask your team. Make sure they point to specific instances, but don't just rehash the past. Ask them to catch you in the act. Is the task at hand calling for your immediate input—or are you going on autopilot? How would your team rather see you handle it?

You can catch yourself, too, if you know what to watch for. Check out this list of warning signs:

- *You're never quite satisfied with deliverables.*
- *You often feel frustrated because you would've gone about the task differently.*
- *You laser in on the details and take great pride and/or pain in making corrections.*
- *You constantly want to know where all your team members are and what they're working on.*
- *You ask for frequent updates on where things stand.*
- *You prefer to be cc'd on emails.*[23]

The difference between managing and micromanaging is compulsion. Of course, you cannot blindly trust people to do the job right. They need to earn your trust. Until they do, you need to stay on top of projects and pay attention to detail. The question is—*is it possible for another person to satisfy you?* If your record says, "not really," it means that you check on people compulsively, whether or not it's necessary, and even when it makes things worse.

READY TO QUIT?

If micromanaging is an old mean habit of yours, it won't give up at once. Get help. Let your people coach you—it's your chance to prove that you can take guidance. And it's a great way to restore trust and empower your team.

Daniel H. Pink, the author of *Drive* and a great proponent of autonomy at work, recommends managers take these three steps toward giving up control: (1) involve people in goal setting; (2) use non-controlling language; and (3) hold office hours so people can come see you.

Micromanagement starts in the mind. Pay attention to how you rationalize your need to micromanage. See it for what it really is. Then create a saner approach. The following are some of the most common excuses along with their hidden meanings:[24]

What chronic micromanagers say	What they really mean
It will save me time if I just do it myself	I don't believe its worth my time to let them try because they won't get it right anyway
Too much is at stake to allow this to go wrong	I don't trust them to do their jobs according to my standards
It's my credibility on the line if they don't get it done on time	The work won't get done unless I constantly prod them
When I am not involved they mess up	The one time I yielded some control there was a mistake and I'm not willing to take that risk again
My boss wants me to be heavily involved in my team's work	If I don't stay involved, how else will I prove my worth?

If you buy into your excuses, your only two options are; micromanage or fail, which, of course, is not true. Anyone can delegate just about anything successfully. Just make sure you ask questions upfront to see that people are well matched to the tasks. If they aren't, no amount of handholding will get you the result you need. Define your checkpoints carefully, and let them come to you for help. Don't panic if they take off in the wrong direction; you can always reassign the whole project or redistribute individual tasks. Keep in mind that "different" doesn't always mean "wrong." Stay open to the multiple ways of getting the job done, and, where possible, let them choose their own path.

Ultimately, micromanagement is only an imperfect substitute for those human relationships and working conditions that make it easy for people to do the job right. If peeking over your people's shoulders hasn't paid off, try generosity and trust.

SAS was no. 2 (behind Google) on *Fortune's* "100 Best Companies to Work For" in 2014. The statistical software company is famous for its thirty-eight-year history of revenue growth, surpassing $3 billion in 2014. It's equally famous for investing in its people. SAS headquarters in Cary, North Carolina, boasts a massive sports and fitness complex, free on-site health care, and deeply discounted childcare.

Not only do SAS employees get unlimited access to company facilities, they get to choose when to use them. Everyone sets his own hours. Like other companies, SAS has a workweek policy: thirty-five hours or more. What's different is the way they enforce it.

> *I don't know anybody who really works 35 hours. The reality is if you trust people, and you ask them to do something—and you treat them like a human being as opposed to a commodity where you try to squeeze something out—they're going to work all sorts of hours. But they're going to enjoy those hours as opposed to "slaving in the office."* [25]

Micromanagement won't win you any loyalty or enthusiasm from your employees. While some companies gently discourage it, Google took a chainsaw to it:

> *Google gives its rank and file room to make decisions and innovate. Along with that freedom comes a greater respect for technical expertise, skillful problem solving, and good ideas than for titles and*

formal authority. Given the overall indifference to pecking order, anyone making a case for change at the company needs to provide compelling logic and rich supporting data. Seldom do employees accept top-down directives without question.[26]

Engineers are not the only ones enjoying creative freedom at Google. Trust trickles down all the way from the top. Susan Wojcicki, who built Google's advertising business, has the complete trust of CEO Larry Page. As Google folklore puts it, *"What Susan wants, Susan gets."* And with good reason—in 2014 ad sales brought in $59 billion, or 90 percent of the total revenues.

Susan is the boss of Neal Mohan, the VP of display advertising products. She has managed to keep Mohan, despite the competition's constant attempts to hire him away. He could name his price at either Twitter or Facebook. Plus, he could easily make CEO somewhere else. This is why he hasn't:

A source close to Mohan tells us he already feels like CEO, but one who doesn't have to do all the annoying parts of the job … "He's in a really good spot … There is one guy who runs display advertising at Google, and that's Neal. Susan leaves it to him. If he had another display guy above him, or if there were political nonsense going on, he would probably take off sooner. But there isn't."[27]

Absence of micromanagement is a huge competitive advantage. Use it to hold on to good employees at every level. A management philosophy known as ROWE (Results Only Work

Environment) keeps people accountable for work goals and removes all other constraints: no expected time in the office, dress code or unnecessarily standardized procedures. Jody Thompson and Cali Ressler pioneered ROWE at Best Buy. Now Gap, Inc. and other companies have adopted it to create trust-based high-performing teams.

To speed up the transfer of control from manager to employee, technology has created the virtual workplace. And many employers, like LiveOps from Chapter 5, are eager to kill two birds with one stone: give employees their much-desired space and reap the cost savings of housing fewer bodies.

However, as LiveOps found out, a virtual office doesn't solve the problem of keeping people focused and motivated. It substitutes one driver, autonomy, for another, community. And, since we frequently derive our sense of purpose, mastery, and success from those around us, our motivation suffers.

The solution? Keep connected at all costs. Use technology and common sense to create close working relationships up, down, and across your organization. This actually means fewer conference calls, not more. Like all meetings, conference calls are mostly an excuse to micromanage—with an added disadvantage of being glued to a screen and having to speak into a void. When you do have them, be brief, never go on mute, and call on people often to share their thoughts. Don't give overly detailed instructions. Let people ask questions and figure it out for themselves.

Expect meetings to disappear, as individuals and groups hit "the zone," and everyone knows what to do without being told. Then watch them reappear—because people actually enjoy working together.

Micromanagement loads your to-do list with other people's jobs. And, although most managers will be thrilled to lighten up their load, some fear they won't have enough. Don't worry! There is more to management than being a taskmaster. Your team desperately needs you for things only you can do. Here's Stephanie Davis, another winner of Google's Great Manager Award:

> *Personally, I have always been inspired by Eric [Schmidt], Larry, and Sergey; I thought my team was also getting a sense of the company's vision from them. But this survey gave my team the opportunity to explain that they wanted me to interpret the higher-level vision for them. So I started listening to the company's earnings call with a different ear. I didn't just come back to my team with what was said; I also shared what it meant for them.*[28]

If your inner micromanager shows up at the office, it's wise to take him on. Overcoming micromanagement, alone, can turn around your relationship with any individual employee—or the whole team. What's more, once your insecurity lets up, your best and most powerful self can step in and take charge.

CHAPTER 12
BE AUTHENTIC

❝You can make an ordinary situation funny by substituting honesty where, ordinarily, people would lie or avoid saying anything. Honesty in social situations is so rare that it automatically qualifies as bizarre. And it's usually cruel too. You get two of the six dimensions of humor—bizarre and mean—without much effort. ❞

— SCOTT ADAMS, *The Joy of Work*

❝What makes Pixar special is that we acknowledge we will always have problems, many of them hidden from our view; that we work hard to uncover these problems, even if doing so means making ourselves uncomfortable; and that, when we come across a problem, we marshal all of our energies to solve it. ❞

— ED CATMULL, Creativity, Inc.

When we manage other people, we naturally want to be taken seriously. We worry about their opinion of us, and we work hard to project an image that is sure to command respect.

Is it a good strategy? Does a closely guarded persona elevate the boss in the eyes of his subordinates?

BlessingWhite says no. In fact, the opposite is true. In one survey, employees rated their immediate managers on eight critical skills. The survey also asked whether they knew the manager well as a person. Researchers wanted to see if a personal relationship with the manager influenced the employee's professional opinion of him or her. They found out that—

Managers who put up a front scored, on average, 59 percent lower than those who showed their human side.

Here's what the results look like for North America, skill by skill:[29]

I believe that my manager ...	% of people that know their manager well and agree	% of people that don't know their manager well and agree
Has built a sense of belonging in our department.	66%	18%
Recognizes and rewards my achievements.	73%	25%
I have a great working relationship with my manager.	83%	31%
Treats me like an individual with unique interests and needs.	82%	37%
Provides me with regular, specific feedback on my performance.	59%	21%
Encourages me to use my talents as much as possible.	79%	35%
Asks for and acts on my input.	81%	37%
Delegates assignments without micromanaging.	78%	47%

Of the eight skills included in the survey, the top four are "soft," or relationship-building skills. The bottom four are a typical manager's job duties. However, no matter what skill you picked, employees overwhelmingly favored those managers whom they thought they knew well. Take a basic business skill, like delegation, for example. A total of 78 percent of those employees who said they knew their manager as a person approved of his delegating abilities, vs. only 47 percent of those reporting to a stranger. What, then, can you expect of a touchy feely metric, like *"My manager has built a sense of belonging"*? Stuffed shirts need not apply: 66 percent vs. 18 percent, in favor of the human manager!

The results also varied by engagement levels. The less engaged the employees were, the higher they ranked those managers with whom they had built a personal connection. For the least engaged, the average gap in the rankings was 63 percent.

The message is simple, if often overlooked. *There is no such thing as impersonal work relationships.* Especially between the manager and his direct reports. It is the manager's ability to authentically connect with people that earns him respect and empowers him to do his job.

In 2013, Gallup published its widely quoted *State of the Global Workplace* report, according to which 71 percent of North American and 87 percent of worldwide employees are *"not engaged"* or *"actively disengaged."* Add the fact that disengaged employees are also the ones most sensitive to "inauthentic" bosses—and showing your human side becomes the gold mine of employee engagement.

Let me say that again.

> *Showing your human side is the gold mine of employee engagement.*

Why, then, don't more managers give it a try? BlessingWhite offers this insight:

> *While companies focus on equipping managers with tactical skills such as delegation or matching individual talents to tasks, engagement is driven more effectively through leadership and connection skills. Particularly difficult for a manager is the challenge of authenticity—because they are typically being taught how to behave, how to "play a role". In actual fact, it's becoming better known as a person to their direct reports—not being the person they think they ought to be—that will build the relationship needed to increase engagement.*[30]

What is all this role-playing? And why do we learn it in the first place? Here's a problem with being authentic. You could be a world-class asshole.

SO YOU'RE HIGHLY UNLIKEABLE ...

One Steve Jobs story says he was fond of asking random employees what they were working on. One question led to another—and failure to briefly and eloquently state your case could get you fired on the spot. For this reason, everyone at Apple knew Steve's lunch hour and cleared the patio where he liked to sit down and eat fifteen to twenty minutes ahead of time.

Another way to arouse Jobs' curiosity was to run into him in an elevator. Seasoned employees knew to duck at the sight of him approaching the elevator lobby. But some of the newbies had to learn the hard way. When cornered in an elevator, one intern said he was doing quality assurance for a product. "Then why are you going down?" asked Jobs. "You should be going back to your desk to work." The kid was preparing for the worst, but the boss was in a playful mood. "Hey, just kidding."

Even in extreme cases of bad personality, however, some would argue for the "devil that you know." If people know what to expect from you, they can prepare. They could even help you get better. Unless, of course, they are deathly afraid of you.

Showing your feelings doesn't mean indulging your abusive streak. Anger, whether or not we allow it to surface, is only a cover-up for another deeply felt emotion. Usually, something rather opposite in nature. Insecurity? Doubt? Fear? Do you know yours? Do you own your feelings? If not to employees, then at least to yourself?

Sheryl Sandberg's job as Facebook's second-in-command was never easy. Lawsuits. Intense public scrutiny. Controversy over going to China. In 2012, *Time* magazine named Sandberg among its 100 most influential people in the world. How does she stand up to all that pressure?

> *I've cried at work. I've cried to Mark. He was great. He was, like, "Do you want a hug? Are you O.K.?"*[31]

SHOW YOUR VULNERABILITY

We think we know how people would respond, when, in reality, our entire past experience with them has been a result of our own attitudes. When we change the way we relate to people, their response changes dramatically. Be honest about your struggles and let them surprise you with their empathy and good will.

You don't need a crisis or a special occasion to be human. Use your real self every day, for both work and play. We often worry that our personalities will get in the way of our work relationships. Strangely enough, people like to know each other by their quirks. It makes them more comfortable in their own skin.

Trust your people to know you as a person. You will find them a lot more responsive than if you just rely on your official capacity as manager. You will find yourself more responsive to them, too. Trust is usually reciprocated. And being trusted makes everyone more willing to do the work, no matter what kind of work it is.

When insecurity strikes, resist the temptation to cover it up. Speak your mind and make it okay for everyone to do the same. For example, if you are feeling silent tension in the room, don't explain it away in your head. Ask what's going on. What is everyone thinking and not saying?

You may be asking yourself, do I really want to know? Make sure the answer is yes. You will find it difficult to be real with people unless everyone follows suit. Watch out for the quiet resenters and the yes-men (of both genders). Don't gloss over inauthentic behaviors. Instead, prove it to them that opening up to you is worth the risk.

SETTING THE TONE IS NOT ENOUGH

Praise people for being honest and direct to dispel their fear of being criticized. Their second greatest fear is usually not being heard. They will be watching you closely to see if you listen—or care. Dismiss or minimize their pet issues, and you've failed the test. It doesn't matter if you do it subtly or bluntly, intentionally or inadvertently.

The only way to earn their trust is to get what they are saying and why it's important to them. Listen from their mindset, not yours. Ask clarifying questions. Remember, it's just as important to leave them feeling heard and understood, as it is to hear and understand on your end. Don't worry about agreeing or disagreeing with them and don't let it derail your conversation. Focus on getting everything on the table. Once again, you'll be shocked at how easy it is to move forward when there are no emotional minefields to cross.

While we're on the subject of being authentic, let's not forget the basics: keep your promises and don't lie. To most people, this is a moral principle they learned growing up. I was no different. I had heard it often from my parents, my Boy Scout leaders, and when playing sports. However, I had to learn it a second time as a business skill. And the full credit goes to my former business partner, "Modest Gabe."

One time Gabe and I were out bidding on a software project for a local business. At the end of our pitch, the business owner started asking questions, all the standard stuff everyone wants to know.

> BUSINESS OWNER: How long have you been in business?
> MODEST GABE: Three years. (Fact: We had had our company for six months and had known each other for a total of a year and a half.)
> BUSINESS OWNER: I see. How many customers do you have?
> MODEST GABE: Twenty-three customers. (Fact: One.)
> BUSINESS OWNER: I see. How many employees do you have?
> MODEST GABE: Seventy-five employees. (Fact: He was looking at it.)
> BUSINESS OWNER: Thank you for coming out. Let me get back to you.

The business owner was expecting *some* BS, within the bounds of reasonable and customary. "Seventy-five employees" hit it out of the ballpark and cost us the job. There was clearly more to the art of misrepresenting yourself than blatant disregard of the facts. If anyone wants to become a better liar, I can recommend Paul Ekman's *Telling Lies,* a book used to catch professional liars, like drug dealers and spies.

Long story short, I decided I didn't want to be a professional liar. That meant I needed a new strategy for attracting and retaining customers. My strategy was not only to avoid telling boldface lies, but also to keep promises I made out of ignorance and desperation. And I made a lot of those early on.

A month after Vivek and I started Axero, we landed our second customer. Luigi was a stockbroker from Las Vegas who spoke with a thick Brooklyn accent. True to form, Luigi was never happy with our work, no matter how hard we tried to please him. He kept us on the phone for hours, cursing and making death threats. All of our subcontractors bailed out. Vivek and I sucked it up and finished the job.

We never got a thank you note from Luigi. Instead, we gained self-respect as a company: if nothing else, we had our word to offer. Over time, other customers have rewarded us for honoring tough commitments. And, since we are the good guys, we go a little beyond what we've promised, like refunding the monthly fee when people sign up for Communifire and don't use it. *Here, Mr. Customer, take your $50 back. We want you to feel good about your business with us.*

You know who really appreciates being treated like a real human being by another human being? Your customers. Apparently it's still rare in the business world, and people are making all kinds of money, just by being human at work. Take the world-famous CEO of Zappos, Tony Hsieh, for example.

Tony's been in the news ever since 2009, when Amazon acquired Zappos for $1.2 billion. He is a leading authority on both employee happiness and commercial success. Initially, Tony was skeptical about the idea of selling shoes online. If there's one product you absolutely must try before you buy it, it's shoes. Because when shoes don't fit, it's a big problem. Tony realized that the only way to overcome this disadvantage is with outrageously friendly and helpful customer service. Finding, exchanging, and returning shoes at Zappos would not only have to be as convenient as it is at any brick-and-mortar store, it would have to be better. Easier, less stressful, and more than that—encouraging, refreshing, and exciting!

Tony's strategy was a huge success. In 2000, its second year, Zappos sold $1.6 million worth of shoes. In 2008, the sales reached $1 billion. During this time, Tony has searched high and low to find out what helps his people "deliver happiness" to his customers. Here's what he believes lies at the core:

> *So many people when they go to the office, they leave a little bit of themselves at home, or a lot of themselves at home. And while there's been a lot of talk over the years about work life separation or work life balance, our whole thing is about work life integration. Because it's just life—and the ideal would be if you can be the same person at home as you are in the office and vice versa.*[32]

CHAPTER 13
HELP

❝ I think my most important job in IBM is working with anybody who has a problem. ❞

— THOMAS WATSON, JR., second president of IBM (1952–1971)

❝ Your boss has a deep psychological need to feel that he has 'helped.' Unfortunately, the quantity of 'help' that your boss provides will have no correlation to his abilities or your needs. ❞

— SCOTT ADAMS, *The Joy of Work*

Anyone who has ever tried being human with people has invariably made an astounding discovery. Other people are human too! They want to do a good job and make you happy. Sometimes they succeed on their own. Other times they need help.

Help is like medicine. It's not enough to treat the symptoms. You must recognize the root cause and treat the whole patient. For the manager, this means focusing on the problem the employee is struggling with internally, not just the one he is creating for you.

Let me give you an example. Remember Axero's long-suffering outsourced blog? Once I figured that editing it would be a full-time job, I did what most managers would do in my place. I fired the writing company and hired a single in-house writer who would focus on my blog and give me exactly what I needed.

What I needed were in-depth captivating articles of two thousand words or more on the topics of my choosing. After a year of working with us, the writer still hadn't written a single piece that didn't take me hours to edit. The worst part were the endless dependent clauses, empty adjectives and repetitions serving no other purpose than to fluff up a paragraph's worth of useful word count. For example, instead of *"Every company needs an intranet,"* he'd write, *"There is no getting around the fact that every company, no matter how big or small or what kind of business it is in, or where it is located, needs to have a viable intranet, where employees can access different kinds of information pertinent to their jobs."*

I felt cheated and annoyed, and I was getting ready to cut him loose. Vivek, Bryce, and Trevor gave me their unanimous blessing. ("This is bullshit, man. Get rid of him.") On the other hand, he'd never missed a deadline, and we had just spent a year teaching him about our business. Where was the guarantee that the next writer would give us what we were after? I asked myself if there was anything I could have done differently to help him write better posts. And there was plenty.

As much as I loathed his tumorous sentences, I had never confronted him face-to-face. I just cleaned them up when I had time—or posted them as-is when I didn't. So, I called him up and ripped apart two or three of his posts. I said, "Look, I can't use these. We need to cut out the fluff and tighten the message. Can you do it?"

It turned out that he could. He just needed some talking points for each article. He was having trouble coming up with his own material but was reluctant to ask me for help. He was a very hard worker who stood by his promises. Hence all the word magic that had nearly cost him his job.

I was more than happy to give talking points, especially if that meant no more editing. Brain dumping was never a problem for me. Wake me up in the middle of the night, give me a topic, and I will surprise both of us with the sheer volume of facts and angles immediately popping into my head. To me, it was the easiest part of his job, which is why I hadn't offered to help him with it. To him, it was the hardest—which is, probably, why he hadn't asked.

This brings us to the heart of being a manager. What do you do when you are no longer only responsible for yourself, but for other people, too? Everyone has different needs. How do you address them all without micromanaging the daylights out of people? The key is where you focus. Micromanagers focus on their own need to stay in control. They repeatedly answer their own questions, which come from their own past and create anxiety in their own minds. This is why micromanagement doesn't help.

When we shift the focus to others, we may realize we don't even know how to help them. This is a good start. It leads the manager to stop answering the wrong questions and start asking the right ones. Sometimes, that's all the help the employee needs.

When asking questions, aim to help the employee find his own solution, not solve the problem for him. Pretend you are talking to someone more competent than yourself. The fact is people are the utmost experts on what's going on in their heads. Your job is simply to prompt them to put all that knowledge to good use. There are different ways you can do that, both verbal and non-verbal.

FIRST THINGS FIRST: YOUR ATTITUDE IS KEY

Don't even try to help people, unless you care about them. Get personal. Recognize that there is a human being in front of you. Think: *give him a break*, not: *put him on the spot*. If people are struggling at work, they are probably already feeling a lot of pressure. Put them at ease and give them the confidence to show what they know. As a manager, you have the awesome power to release people from their insecurities. Use it.

How exactly do you encourage and empower people when they have just disappointed you? Excellent question. A lot of managers play the good-news-bad-news game to ease into a sore subject. I prefer to put business aside altogether and have a good ol' small talk to get people to relax and feel good about themselves. Of course, you have to be open and relaxed yourself. Otherwise, you'll sound like you are beating around the bush, and you'll make the employee even more nervous.

WHAT KIND OF A RELATIONSHIP ARE YOU CREATING?

Let's say you are calling to find out what's holding up a project. No matter how important the project is, your relationship with people who work for you is the bigger picture. Solving the problem by damaging the relationship is like winning a battle, but losing the war. Don't let it happen. For example, I never start a call with, "What's the status of project X?" I wouldn't want people to tense up every time they see my name pop up on the screen. "The boss is calling to chew me out!" Whatever is going on, the call is still an opportunity to catch up and show that I care. I'd say:

"How are things going?"

"What did you do this weekend? Anything fun?"

"How's the family/wife/kids/pets?"

"What else is new?"

I like to let the conversation naturally flow into work talk.

"So, what do you have going on today?" (Let them talk.)

"Anything I can help you with?" (Let them talk.)

"Any challenges you are facing?"

"Would you like to run through what you've done so far? Would it be helpful to talk it through?"

For the most part, I am religiously open-ended. Of course, the most open-ended thing to do in a conversation is to say nothing at all and let the other person fill in the pause. It usually gets people to show you what's on their minds. Sometimes it's a lot of ranting and excuses. And that's okay too. They need to let it out before they can start making sense again. The best way to help them in that moment is to listen and let the conversation be about them. Don't turn the tables and make it about you.

TRY ACTIVE LISTENING

Volumes have been written on active listening. If this is a new subject for you, take a look at *Active Listening 101: How to Turn Down Your Volume to Turn Up Your Communication Skills* by Emilia Hardman.

In a nutshell, active listening is listening to another person with the intention to understand rather than educate or change his mind. It's a little like learning a foreign language. You repeat back what you heard, to make sure you got it right. Not just facts, but also feelings. For example, if the employee seems frustrated, say, "It really bothers you that I did X," and listen carefully for him to confirm or deny your impression.

If you've never done it before, it takes a little practice to get it right. Don't play the therapist and don't parrot every single word. The last thing people want when they are in a jam is to be lab rats for some sort of a technique. Do let them know that you hear them. And paraphrase *some* things they say to show that you get it.

When talking face-to-face, remember that your body is doing most of the talking. Don't hover over people, sit down with them. Look them in the eye and give them your full attention. Nod your head when they nod. Smile when they smile.

KEEP THE LINES OPEN

A helpful and compassionate attitude will lead you to uncover a hidden roadblock faster than a demanding one. When you reach out to help, your actions say "we are in this together," a far more uplifting message than "you've dropped the ball."

Let people know they can come to you whenever they feel uncertain or stuck, to avoid problem-solving after the fact. Whether or not they actually do it is partly their work style and partly yours. As a minimum, take these steps to "keep the lines open": (1) Be on the radar. Show your face. Answer questions. Get involved in day-to-day life. Chitchat. (2) Respond. Pick up your phone. Answer your email. If you promise something—to get information or to put people in touch—don't make them wait. (3) Show interest. Nobody wants to be a pest. People won't come to you for help if they feel their project is second-rate and isn't worth your time.

Not everyone knows when they need help. And not everyone who knows it feels comfortable asking. At Axero, we set the bar really low, especially with the new hires. Ask even if you are 100 percent sure of the answer. Ask everyone the same question over and over again. There is always a lot of back-and-forth the first few months. After that, they sync up with the team, and the conversations become normal.

Will your people grow helpless and overly dependent if you make yourself unconditionally available for help on projects? That depends on the kind of help you give. If you substitute your skills for theirs, chances are they'll keep bringing their work to you. However, if you show trust in their abilities, leave room for mistakes, and help them build confidence, you'll train them to make good calls on their own.

Bottom line: be generous towards your people. Don't draw the line in the sand between their problems and yours. And don't value your own effort above theirs. When you are willing and ready to give of yourself, your presence clears the air and makes a solution possible.

Companies spend a lot of time and money trying to figure out systematic ways of dealing with employees. It seems like there is a protocol and an IT solution for just about any workplace issue. However, even the best system cannot account for all eventualities. As a human being, you have the ability to feel other people's pain. And as a manager, you have the power to relieve it.

CHAPTER 14

REWARD LIKE A KING

" A ruler should be slow to punish and swift to reward. "
— OVID

" Being the richest man in the cemetery doesn't matter to me ... Going to bed at night saying we've done something wonderful ... that's what matters to me. "
— STEVE JOBS

You work hard as a manager. That's how you get to be one in the first place. So, from time to time, it's nice to see some appreciation. Not just from the higher-ups, but from the people with whom you spend most of your workday: your staff.

Unfortunately, employee love and enthusiasm are hard to come by. Here's the Biggest Challenge at Work again, and a chorus of managers who aren't feelin' it from the teams:

Job Title	Biggest Challenge at Work
Divisional Manager	"Lack of passion. Legacy issues. Change."
Owner	"Managing people"
Business Dev. Manager	"Morale"
HR Manager	"Morale"
Team Manager	"Morale"

Director of Operations	"Retention"
Business Manager	"Staff retention"

Oftentimes, it's not even the manager's fault. Like it says above, it could be a legacy issue. It could also be a company-wide or an industry-wide problem, bad economy, healthcare crisis ... Whatever is weighing people down, it's the manager's job to get them excited about work again. So there's got to be something you can do.

How about everything we've talked about so far? Have you found your issue yet? Have you made it better? Many problems go away when you use people the right way, support careers, give visibility, don't micromanage, talk and act like a real human, and reach out to help. But what if you are already doing all of those things? Is it possible that something is still missing from your relationship with your crew?

I think the answer is yes. All of the above are fundamental to being a good boss. And, like all fundamentals, your good-boss ethics are apt to be taken for granted—along with the free coffee and biweekly direct deposit. And yet, unless the relationship with the boss (you) feels *rewarding* to people day-to-day, like any relationship, it grows stale.

Rewards are different from regular pay, benefits and perks, in that they go above and beyond. The point of a reward is not to take care of all employees equally, but to single out a few and make them feel special. It works because human beings are insatiable approval seekers. We are not happy until someone praises us and marvels at our handiwork. We need lots and lots of approval every day. And, as long as there's some hope of winning it, we are willing to try again and again.

Be selective with your approval, but when you do give it, show that you mean it. Ancient kings used the full range of their power to reward loyal service. It was a royal prerogative to bestow lands, titles, honors, and even the hand of the royal offspring. A king's prerogative went as far as letting the chosen one name his own reward. All for a good reason: rewards keep people busy vying for the king's favor, instead of plotting against him.

Today, rewards are the secret to being a tough boss. Yes, we operate with a different set of carrots, but the principle holds. Your freedom to reward is your best tool for winning loyalty and boosting morale. Fight for it, if you have to.

RECOGNITION IS MORE IMPORTANT THAN PAY

The more effort that goes unrecognized at work, the lower the morale. Aon Hewitt's 2013 report, *Trends in Global Employee Engagement*, lists recognition among the top five drivers of employee engagement in North America. Speaking of taking things for granted, pay didn't even make the shortlist.

Competitive pay is a must for attracting and retaining good people. Yet, when it comes to reinforcing behaviors, money has a few disadvantages. First, the satisfaction it delivers is short-lived. Second, money never makes up for lack of intrinsic motivation. You simply cannot pay people enough to like their job. Finally, perceived pay inequity makes for a very toxic workplace. It's better to pay similarly for similar jobs, and reward outstanding contributions by other means.

The most important thing you can do as a boss is to notice and reward effort. If you don't do it, who will? Top management is not there day-to-day. Customers come and go.

Besides, not every employee is in a customer-facing job. Some companies have peer recognition systems in place. (We'll talk about these in Chapter 23, *Say Thank You.*) If yours is one of these companies, great! You are ahead of the game. However, a company-wide program doesn't replace rewarding your team in your own special way. Because that's how you build your own special relationships with them.

You probably want to know what kinds of rewards I have in mind. You are waiting to see if I am going to suggest something boring, like gift cards, or something dumb, like naming a conference room after the employee of the month. Fair enough. I will have a list for you at the end of the chapter. But first, to me, rewards are less about being creative and more about knowing what people really need and appreciate. Money can play a role, but it's only half of the solution. The other half is making a difference in people's lives. If you know a sure way of doing that, then go ahead and spend the money for them.

Case in point: When we promoted Raghav to lead architect, we gave him a substantial raise. We thought we had done great by him, until one day Vivek dropped by his place. Broken windows. Seedy neighborhood. Raghav was so absorbed in his work that he didn't bother about his surroundings. We bought him a new apartment, furnished it, and moved him in. Today, Raghav can have a job anywhere he wants. But he is still an Axero man. It's personal.

On the flip side, recognizing and rewarding top performers is a fantastic opportunity to piss people off. Which doesn't mean that you shouldn't do it. It only means that you need to think it through and put yourself in the shoes of both the winners and the losers. If you don't, you risk getting the exact opposite of what you wish for. Here's what happened to my brother.

The ad agency where he worked ran ad-of-the-month contests. The three best designs earned cash prizes. When my brother won his first contest, he was really excited. He called me and bragged about it. The next month, his was again the best ad in the agency. This time, however, it won nothing, not even a third place. The next month it was the same. My brother was perplexed. He showed me the winning ads and asked if he was a narcissistic prick unable to appreciate other people's talents. He was not. He just happened to be hands-down their best designer. In six months he was out of there.

What happened? The ad agency had nothing against my brother. On the contrary, they were full of good intentions. They wanted to spread the wealth and make other designers feel good about themselves. They figured my brother would understand and others would go along. Instead, the contest became a joke. Management lost credibility. And the agency lost a key employee.

They did have a point, though. Anytime you single someone out for a prize, someone else is bound to feel left out. However, their solution was worse than the problem. Arbitrarily excluding my brother from consideration invalidated the reward scheme and defeated the purpose.

If you are going to have contests, expect people to feel jealous and question your decisions. It's normal. Do your part by making it clear what the reward is for and how the winners are chosen. If you don't want the same people to win twice in a row, say so upfront. Then leave it up to your crew to respond graciously. And always create new opportunities to win.

REWARD WITH PURPOSE

Rewards don't need to be competitive to set a strong example. You can reward every individual who achieves a certain result. Or reward the whole team for completing a critical project. Some managers like to reward spontaneously. Others do it methodically, to focus the team on success factors and solve persistent problems. Do you know what kinds of behaviors you want to promote within your team? Here are some ideas.

- **Product releases** (and version releases, in the software world). These are a huge strain on everybody and will always be, no matter what project management and quality assurance system you use. Celebrate and reward every one, and your people will embrace the fact that they make a hard living, instead of resenting it.

- **Safety.** If accidents are a problem, reward people at the end of every accident-free week, month, quarter, or year.

- **Long service.** In 1924, IBM's president Thomas J. Watson started the Quarter Century Club, to recognize employees with twenty-five years of service. Much has changed since then. Today, many employees feel the pressure to job-hop or retire early. However, if you are fortunate enough to have a loyal employee on your team, don't let this fact go unnoticed.

- **Meeting goals.** IBM was also one of the first employers to realize that people need to feel good about meeting their goals, in order to set new, even more ambitious ones. In 1925, the first meeting of the Hundred

Percent Club, composed of IBM salesmen who meet their quotas, convened in Atlantic City.

- **Being a model employee.** Remember Google's eight key behaviors for the front-line manager? After working hard to figure out what kinds of managers it wanted, Google established the Great Manager Award. To get the award, the manager must be nominated by his subordinates and selected by the committee.

- **Goofy anti-achievements.** Do you want to have fun and recognize some quirky habits among the team? Come on, we are all human. Besides, accepting one's faults is the first step to change. How about the Best Napper award for someone who likes to snooze in meetings? Or a Yes-But trophy for the resident contrarian?

Once you know *what* you want to recognize your people for, the question is *how*. As promised, I have a few case studies and examples on that front, too. Just remember that it's the people, not the awards, that need to feel valued, special and unique. And, that there are both easy and hard ways of going about it.

- **Friday drinks.** Take your team out to celebrate on a Friday afternoon. Do they have a favorite hangout? Leave early, so people don't have to stay after work—or bring food and drinks into the office and give the rest of the day off.

- **Time off.** Celebrate making a deadline or completing a project by giving your team extra time to recharge and spend with their loved ones.

- **Subsidized sports and fitness activities.** Why not support healthy habits in your best (if not all) people? Gym passes, walking, running, and cycling events, or amateur sports are all great rewards to those who will use them.

- **Personal and career development.** Everyone can use a little training and coaching to take their game to the next level. There are great courses out there that benefit the whole person, as well as a specific career. If this is not an option for everyone on your team, use it selectively to invest in your top performers.

- **Hanging out with top brass.** Do your people spend enough face time with you and other big shots at your company? If you offer yourself as a prize, don't repeat the mistake I made with Bryce. Make sure the setting is comfortable and the employee feels relaxed in your company. Google puts its Great Manager Award winners on a plane to Hawaii, where they get to spend a week side-by-side with senior execs.

- **Visibility.** Yes, we've already covered this, but it's worth repeating. Do your people like to see their names in bright lights? Most social intranet platforms have built-in leader boards. We use ours to show who's answered the most questions for customers. (Bryce, usually.)

- **Stuff.** Let people pick out free stuff from your e-commerce site. If you don't have one, it's easy to set up.

- **Everyone's favorites.** Are your people hooked on Starbucks or Netflix? Do you have a lot of pet owners around the office? People cherish thoughtful gifts more than expensive ones. Show employees that you know and care about them as people. Try personalized gift cards, chew toys for animals, a book they've been wanting to read—or anything else you know they'll love.

Every side of the manager-employee relationship we've discussed in this part of the book is *personal*. It's negotiated human being to human being, even though it falls under the work contract. Rewards are no different. And therein lies their exceptional power to motivate. As a manager, you may or may not have a say over how much money your people make. Don't let that limit your personal power to reward good work.

One company has used this principle to build its entire brand. The East Coast grocery chain Wegmans is one of the lesser-known names on *Fortune's* 100 Best Companies to Work For. In 2014, it placed at no. 12, outranking such iconic retailers as Whole Foods and REI.

Even if you didn't know that almost half of Wegmans employees are twenty-five or younger, you probably guessed that money wasn't the main draw here. Rather, the company rewards employees with flexible scheduling, college scholarships, trips around the world to learn about products, and stretch assignments to help young employees grow within the company. As a result, Wegmans' turnover is an incredible 4 percent, compared to 15 percent at Whole Foods, and up to 100 percent in the grocery sector. Wegmans also fills two-thirds of its job openings through internal promotions.

Like Zappos, Wegmans exists to delight the customer. Remarkably, managers and supervisors are not the only ones rewarding great customer service. Employees are encouraged to reward each other with store-paid gift cards. Another subtle perk is the ability to get a job for someone you care about. Wegmans gladly hires family and friends. In fact, family referrals are so frequent that one out of every five employees has a relative working for the company.

From interviewing candidates to watching over careers to dishing out rewards, a boss' work is never done. Wouldn't it be nice if some of it took care of itself, like gift cards at Wegmans, or on-the-job coaching at Best Collateral? Every one of us has seen many examples of employees bossing themselves. The question is: how can companies seize on this trend and turn it on high volume?

The answer is the whole of Part Three: *Empower the Culture.*

PART THREE
EMPOWER THE CULTURE

  ❝ Long ago he formed an ideal conception of omnipotence and omniscience which he embodied in his gods. Whatever seemed unattainable to his desires—or forbidden to him—he attributed to these gods. One may say, therefore, that these gods were the ideals of his culture. **❞**

    — SIGMUND FREUD, *Civilization and Its Discontents*

  ❝ Planet, species, race, nation, state, religion, party, union, club, association, neighborhood improvement committee; I have no interest in any of it. I love and treasure individuals as I meet them, I loathe and despise the groups they identify with and belong to. **❞**

    — GEORGE CARLIN, *Brain Droppings*

  ❝ We seldom realize, for example that our most private thoughts and emotions are not actually our own. For we think in terms of languages and images which we did not invent, but which were given to us by our society. **❞**

    — ALAN WILSON WATTS

CHAPTER 15
AN EXECUTIVE'S VIEW: A COMPANY OF PEOPLE

" You couldn't fault managers for reaching the conclusion that employee happiness and stock prices are inversely related. The evidence was impossible to ignore:

Things That Make Employees Unhappy	Result
Downsizing	Stock goes up
Reduced benefits	Stock goes up
Unpaid overtime	Stock goes up
Doubling the workload	Stock goes up "

— SCOTT ADAMS, *The Joy of Work*

" We believe it is easy to be penny wise and pound foolish with respect to benefits that can save employees considerable time and improve their health and productivity. "

— LARRY PAGE, SERGEY BRIN, "An Owner's Manual" for Google's Shareholders

---

Winners get to write history.

Not only do some companies swim in profits and free publicity, they reset the standard for all the rest. I am not just talking about technology, either. I am talking about a business' moral code. And therein lies the basic injustice of all history: we act upon yesterday's ideas of greatness, yet we are called to answer for our actions by those of tomorrow.

It wasn't so long ago that trimming costs was a business' greatest virtue. Every expense had to be justified, every dollar counted. You couldn't buy napkins for the coffee room without calculating an ROI first. Companies started thinking of employees as costs. Consequently, employee perks were the first to go, closely followed by the jobs themselves.

While all of this flourished on a mass scale, a directly opposite point of view took root quietly in tech incubators out west, hippie food co-ops down south, and, oh, I don't know, maybe some potato farms in Idaho. The proponents of this view believed that people were not a cost, or an asset, or any other accounting item. They believed that people were the company.

Just to be clear, I am not saying the idea of taking care of one's employees is anything new. In 1958, Thomas Watson, Jr., IBM's second CEO, said to his workers, *"This is a company of human beings not machines, personalities not products, people not real estate."* His speech was part of the announcement that, from then on, every U.S. hourly employee at IBM would be paid a salary.

Because IBM was the first large-scale manufacturer to do away with hourly wages, Tom Jr. didn't know if the move would motivate people to work harder or to slack off. Years later he recalled that *"The joke went around that on the first day of hunting season no one would show up for work at our Rochester, Minnesota plant."*

The IBM experiment went well. Employee-friendly policies ahead of its time have kept the company union-free in the U.S. and most places abroad. During the fifteen years that Thomas

Watson, Jr. was in charge, the number of IBM employees qua-drupled, and the revenues grew tenfold. *Fortune* magazine called him *"the greatest capitalist who ever lived."* However, his idea of taking care of employees unconditionally and without regard to their rank didn't catch on until SAS, Google, Zappos and others built vast fortunes doing precisely that and more.

Why did these executives break with convention? What did they see that others didn't? If you ask me, the executive view starts all the way back in Chapter 1, where we talked about the employee and his dilemma. Understanding the way your people think is critical, because you need people to carry out your strategies and think of all the things you hadn't thought of, even though you are a very, very, very smart person. And it's one thing to hire brilliant and congenial people, and quite another to actually get them to use their brains and good will to benefit the company. You can try it the carroty-sticky old-school way, with rules, contracts, fear and pressure. Or you can just get rid of the whole dilemma. Let them feel like they are the company, and let them work the way they like to work. If you do it right, they may not even resent the fact that you are making more money than they are. Happy people don't resent their superiors.

Taking care of people starts with providing for their basic needs and comforts, but it doesn't end there. Companies who choose to focus on employees see a monumental shift in man-agement tactics:

> *Transparency in place of the proverbial "need to know."*
>
> *Listening to employees in place of corporate propaganda.*

And—at the risk of sounding preachy—

A shared purpose in place of elaborate policy-making.

We will examine each one of these in depth later on. But before we do, let's agree that these are, indeed, lasting trends.

Why is all of this happening now? You can go read a bunch of reports on Generation X and Generation Y, and what they will and will not do for a buck. Or you can observe the people around you. I am an X. My brother is a Y. You already know about me. And my brother is even less likely than I to spend the prime of his life in a *Dilbert* cartoon. Why? Because he doesn't have to. He can work for me. For my company, Axero, if you want to take that literally, or for any of my generation of employers—those that don't believe that work should suck.

We were born around the time *work-life balance* became a concern. Our mothers were the first generation of women to choose both family *and* career. Household chores no longer fell along the gender lines. The result was that both men and women wanted more scheduling flexibility and time off work. Notice that they didn't call it "work-home balance" or "work-family balance." By the '70s and '80s, when the work-life movement gained momentum, we had already taken it for granted that we didn't want to go to work. So much so, that we didn't even think of work as life!

This reminds me of a conversation I had with one of our summer interns. She was doing a great job, and I told her we were ready to hire her permanently come fall. She said she loved the work, but she was concerned about work-life balance. I had to put a fist in my mouth, because I was about to tell her to forget everything I said and take her lousy work and her miserable life as far away from my company as possible.

My own reaction caught me off-guard. Why was I so angry? Well, here's why. If you are responsible for the work environment at your company, shouldn't you be insulted when your employees equate it with death?

In my case, she probably freaked when she saw other people, including "big bosses" like Vivek and myself, making comments and posting project updates around the clock. She figured we didn't have a life and that we were going to make a direct frontal assault on hers.

On second thought, I couldn't fault her for being gun-shy. Even though the life-life movement has made it past the turning point, it is far from being the uncontested champion of working America. Plenty of companies are working the old way. Some are doing so very successfully. And, as long as they do, the same words can mean different things, depending on whose camp you are in.

For example, if you google "work-life balance at Apple," a Glassdoor review entitled *"Need work-life balance!"* comes up at the top of the page:

> *... In some groups, work-life balance is non-existent. Working weekends for months on end is considered part of the job, and the attitude is, if you don't like your job, there are plenty out there who would take it. However, that isn't quite true, because we've been having trouble getting quality interviewees for a while now.*

If you google "work-life balance at Google," a Quora review comes up first that says:

> *Google will let you work as hard as you want. There are food and gyms. You can practically live there. It's a balance you need to maintain from within while doing your job well.*

On the face of it, neither company has work-life balance, but for two different reasons. Apple thinks it owns you—while Google lets you loose to the point where you hardly know what to do with yourself. So you end up overworking by force of habit.

Which company would you rather work for?

The answer to this question is already deciding the winners and the losers in the marketplace. It is likely that the epic battle of Apple vs. Google will come down to the "war on talent." And Google has been long preparing to take the lead by perfecting its HR practices and multiplying its world-famous perks.

In 2008, Google entered the smartphone market with Android, its open source operating system, and became a direct competitor of Apple. In 2010, the sales of Android phones surpassed those of the iPhone.

For the record, I was not the one rushing out to buy an Android phone when they hit the stores. You couldn't find a bigger Apple-head than mine. I had a near-religious experience when I saw my one-year-old niece pick up an iPad, push the home button, swipe her finger to unlock the screen, flip through the apps, tap on Netflix, scroll through the movies, and play her favorite cartoon. To me, that kind of a user interface is genius unsurpassed. But the world was ready for a challenger. In the words of a techie-consumer, *"Android is such a relief from the monotony of Microsoft and prison of Apple."*

In 2009, Google's then-CEO, Eric Schmidt, told *The Economist:*

> *Google has a completely different world model. The Apple view is coherently closed. Ours is the inverse model: the web, openness, all the choices, all the voices. And that experiment is running.*[33]

Whose model is going to win?

At $231 billion in revenues (2015), Apple is the twelfth largest company in the world. Google's revenues are only one-third of Apple's. But Google's ability to employ top talent is the envy of the rest of the tech world. And in May of 2016, Google's market cap has actually surpassed that of Apple.

Can they both win, like they seem to so far? As individual companies, yes. But as workplace philosophies, no way. The very fact that Google exists and thrives is a lethal blow to the hierarchical, totalitarian and slave-driven companies. Who the hell wants to work for them if there is an alternative? It's only a matter of time before they mend their ways or go extinct. The game has changed for everyone, including Google itself. Should its world-famous startup culture dissolve into big company politics, its competitive edge will go next.

I always knew that the future belonged to companies who cared, but I couldn't tell you why—until I heard about *"Leaders Eat Last"* by Simon Sinek. The whole thing is brilliant because it ties work to hormones.

It goes something like this: Primitive societies survived because they created a circle of safety for their members. Our bodies adapted, and we started producing the hormones serotonin and oxytocin to motivate ourselves to take care of one another. As long as the company provides that circle of safety for its people, the system is in balance and work gets done. When the company is selfish, the whole system comes under stress. The stress hormone cortisone shuts off all non-vital functions, including the feel-good social hormones. We stop looking out for one another. Work falls by the wayside, because we are too busy covering our asses with both of our hands. And millions of years of evolution (not to mention the miracle of creation) go to waste, because we can't function as reasonable and responsible human beings—although we sure as hell try to fake it at all costs.

Sinek says stress is bad for business. Is it possible that Apple would have made even more money had Steve Jobs been a nicer person?

Maybe. But the moral is to not single-mindedly focus on the money. Focus on the people: employees, customers, the world. Serve their needs and protect them from ... yourself. Google's founding principle says: *"Don't be evil."* Without it, its scientific HR, its sensational perks—and its clever inventions—are nothing but manipulative plays.

While working on this book, I went to see our Internet marketing provider, Hubspot. I'd heard a lot about Hubspot's award-winning Google-inspired employee practices and decided to see for myself. The office space, enclosed within exposed brick and colonial-style windows, looked more like a microbrewery and contained about the same amount of beer, stacked floor to ceiling in fancy cardboard boxes. Aside from the beer, the kitchen had every combination of sugar and caffeine. The employees looked young and enthusiastic. They could all quote their founder, and—this is where it gets creepy—point you to the exact slide in his corporate manifesto where he talks about the kind of people he wants in his company. I just couldn't tell if everyone was truly happy to work there or required to be happy by the slide #145.

Is it possible to copy Google's success? The company has thought through so many details of its daily living, that there is something in it for everyone. But if you are going to copy Google—or any other company—be sure you copy the right things. These are frequently principles and attitudes, rather than specific actions. So, for example, you might agree with Google and Hubspot that your people are under too much stress and that your job is to comfort them. However, you might not rush out to buy beanbags and M&Ms. Yours might be a completely different way to de-stress your employees.

As for Axero, we are certainly not above copying others. You don't need to be original to be good. As it happened, I got most of my ideas about taking care of employees from a girl called Cinnamon who ran a ceramics shop she named A19.

Today A19 is a thriving business producing one-of-a-kind handmade, hand-painted lighting fixtures. But it wasn't always this way. When I met Cinnamon, she was working (and living) out of an old factory building forty miles east of L.A. It was the so-called Inland Empire of Southern California.

Unlike the coastal parts, the Inland Empire is no beach bum paradise. The temperatures climb into the 100s in the summer and dip into the 30s in the winter. The Inland Empire blossomed on the easy credit of the early 2000s. It took in the invading armies of new homeowners, their 4-wheelers, and their flat-screen TVs. In 2009, when the housing bubble burst, many left, turning whole neighborhoods into ghost towns. Crime soared. You could hear gunshots in broad daylight. Inside, the factory was no better than its neighborhood. It was a dingy, dark space filled with dust and paint fumes. It was also the kind of place where a bootstrapped entrepreneur could get her first break.

At the time, A19 was staffed with immigrants making very low wages. No-shows were a daily event, because people could make more money picking strawberries. Cinnamon herself barely got by, working a side job as a Jazzercise instructor. The only way she could keep her factory running was to make her employees happy with the money she had.

She never missed a chance to tell them they were doing a great job. She threw after-work parties for the families and rented bouncing cages for the kids. She'd randomly buy them gift cards for gas and Walmart, or send them away on trips. One day an employee went missing, and the next day a stray dog showed up. The dog stayed, and they named him Daveed, after the no-show. Then things seemed to turn around for A19. It was no longer a migrant's last resort for a steady job. It became a place that Daveed and his two-legged buddies *chose* for themselves.

You can always get ideas about what it means to take care of people. The best ideas for your company will come from your people themselves. What do they need to let go of stress and focus on what they like about their jobs? For us, it turned out to be something far more prosaic than an office pet.

In the early days of Axero, everyone who worked for the company was a freelancer. It was easier for us. Our people had all the freedom and side perks they wanted, but they were missing something that cubicle-dwellers take for granted: health insurance and W-2s. So we went ahead and bought it for them. We had no idea whether payroll and benefits would ever pay for themselves—or how to measure it after the fact. That wasn't the point, anyway. Even if it didn't, we weren't going to take it away. We went through all those hassles and ate all the expense simply because our people wanted it. It gave them peace of mind.

In the following chapters we will talk *culture* ad nauseam. You will see all sorts of things that work for other companies. It might be tempting to try to buy employee engagement with moderately priced gimmicks. Be careful! The culture you create will automatically reflect your hidden agenda. If your intention is anything other than taking care of people who work for you, they will respond with fakery and BS of their own.

CHAPTER 16
GOT CULTURE?

" If you've heard of any bizarre and annoying practices at other companies, convince your boss to try it at yours. Better yet, make up a bizarre and annoying practice and tell your boss that it's commonly used in all the Fortune 500 companies. "

— SCOTT ADAMS, *The Joy of Work*

" Google is not a conventional company. We do not intend to become one. Throughout Google's evolution as a privately held company, we have managed Google differently. We have also emphasized an atmosphere of creativity and challenge, which has helped us provide unbiased, accurate and free access to information for those who rely on us around the world. "

— LARRY PAGE, SERGEY BRIN, "An Owner's Manual" for Google's Shareholders

---

If the words *corporate* and *culture* used side-by-side turn your stomach, blame two Harvard professors.

Between 1987 and 1991, John Kotter and James Heskett conducted several studies comparing companies that "managed their cultures well" to similar companies that did not. Their findings caught the eye of business people around the world— because the first group made a lot more money than the second.

Here's how the professors did it. They looked at twenty-two different industries and picked eight to twelve biggest competitors from each one. For example …

>   **Airlines:** *American, Continental, Delta, Eastern, Northwest, PanAm, Piedmont, TWA, United, and US Air.*

>   **Computers and office equipment:** *Apple Computers, Control Data, Digital Equipment, Hewlett-Packard, Honeywell, IBM, NCR, Pitney Bowes, Unisys, Wang Laboratories, and Xerox.*

>   **The food group:** *Archer Daniels Midland, Borden, ConAgra, CPC Industries, General Mills, IC Industries, Kraft, Pillsbury, Quaker Oats, Ralston Purina, and Sara Lee.*

Next, they mailed a questionnaire to the top six officers in each company asking them to rate their competitors on the strength of their cultures over the preceding decade (late '70s to early '80s). The questionnaire defined a strong culture as one where *(a) "Managers commonly speak of their company's 'style' or way of doing things"; (b) "The firm has both made its values known through a creed or credo and made a serious attempt to encourage managers to follow them"; and (c) "The firm has been managed according to long-standing policies and practices other than those of just the incumbent CEO."*

Kotter and Heskett used the votes of six hundred executives to rank the cultures of these companies from strongest to weakest. Then they compared the financials of the twelve highest-ranked companies to twenty of their closest competitors from the bottom half of the list. The numbers—compounded over the same time period as the culture ratings—made history. Kotter and Heskett published them in their 1992 book, *Corporate Culture and Performance.*

- Revenue growth: 682% vs. 166%
- Stock price increase: 901% vs. 74%
- Net income increase: 756% vs. 1%
- Job growth: 282% vs. 36%

Leave it to Harvard scholars to point out the obvious:

> *A company where most people have the right idea by default is better off than one where a few get it right by accident.*

Nevertheless, before the book came out, people weren't sure if a strong culture could just as easily lead the company astray. The answer is yes, it can, but you will still make money in the short run. For example, if you don't care about customers, you could become a company of assholes, like Stratton Oakmont. Or, if you don't care about your employees and convince them not to care about themselves, you could become a company of suicidally depressed people, like Foxconn. In both cases you will get reprimanded eventually and will have to go up in smoke (Stratton) or mend your ways (Foxconn). However, if you stay within the bounds of common decency, then a strong culture won't hurt anyone and will help your business a lot!

The other question that has confounded people in the past is this: What should corporate culture be about, if not revenues and costs? In a very short article, "Does corporate culture drive financial performance?" written especially for those who don't want to read the whole book, John Kotter explains that …

> … *strong corporate cultures that facilitate adaptation to a changing world are associated with strong financial results. We found that those cultures highly value employees, customers, and owners and that those cultures encourage leadership from everyone in the firm. So if customer needs change, a firm's culture almost forces people to change their practices to meet the new needs. And anyone, not just a few people, is empowered to do just that.*[34]

So, there's once again your recipe for beating the market and outlasting competitors. Empower your people. But wait a minute, do we tell employees to think for themselves to get the job done, or to march in lockstep to create a "strong culture"?

Both, say two Stanford professors. In *Built to Last*, published in 2009, Jim Collins and Jerry Porras talk about *"preserving the core"* and *"stimulating progress."* The core is a set of principles, an ideological common ground extending from the company's past into the future and across the enterprise. And progress is keeping pace with the times, adapting to changes, serving and anticipating the market. And just so you know, either/or is for losers. Great companies know how to live inside a paradox. Life is both the yin and the yang. Deal with it.

After they have thus straightened you out, Collins and Porras set you on the path to immortal profits. For the first part, preserving the core, simply build a cult-like culture within your company. You will need these four ingredients: (1) *Fervently held ideology"*: believe in something, (2) *"Indoctrination"*: spread the word, (3) *"Tightness of fit"*: don't hire non-believers, and (4) *"Elitism"*: make everyone feel special and work with pride.

This actually works, but you will need a strong sense of self to pull it together. In the words of Howard Schultz, the CEO of Starbucks, *"A great business has to have a conscience. You have to know who you are and who you are not."* And that's hard for people, because we are all pleasers and conformists.

And that's where all the crazy over-the-top stuff comes in. It's a simple and awesome differentiation strategy. There is only so much people are willing to do for perks and paychecks. Those who love the company's ways won't mind overindulging. To them, overstepping the boundaries other companies have put in place will feel like a personal victory. But those just tugging along will reach their limits sooner rather than later.

Here's an East Coast company that has sowed eccentricity to reap fun, happiness, prosperity, and success—at least according to *Fortune* magazine. In 2014, Camden Property Trust was ranked no. 11 on *Fortune's* "100 Best Companies to Work For," above Zappos (no. 38), Whole Foods (no. 44), and REI (no. 69). The company had held top ten spots since 2010 and had posted above-expected returns during that period.

Camden owns apartment buildings in several states. It has roughly 1,700 employees. What do all these people love about filling and maintaining rental properties? Comedy and improvisation! Camden management is made up of fun-loving folk who check in with the staff often to see what everyone really wants. It turns out that Camden employees mainly want three things: (1) *"To see humor in everyday events,"* (2) *"To bring the absurd into the workplace,"* and (3) *"To play practical jokes."*

This last category has expanded into an art form under the current management. Flash mobs. Rigged baking contests. Fighting runaway squirrels. President Keith Oden once launched a multi-stage Nerf rocket attack on an unsuspecting finance meeting. The person who got bombshelled in the middle of his PowerPoint was an outside vendor hoping to make a solid impression as a serious professional. Served him right.

Camden people have no trouble formulating their corporate identity. One employee went on record saying that *"If you aren't willing to participate in singing, dancing or being on a stage in front of your peers at some point during your employment, Camden may not be the place for you."*

Camden loves surprises, and not just the rough kind. In 2013 every non-executive employee received $2,000 as a surprise bonus. The regular perks are not bad, either. Six hundred employees live on Camden properties at a 20 percent discount. And furnished apartments at hot vacation spots are just $20 per night.

Culture doesn't have to be about fun, by the way. That's just one example. USAA has built a strong and generally happy (no. 17 on *Fortune's* list) workplace based on service. Its methods, although different from Camden's, are just as unusual. MREs and combat gear don't belong in the office any more than do Nerf rockets. And yet they've both earned their place because that's how both of these companies get their points across to employees. Camden's antics say: be comfortable around people. While USAA's military gear says: walk a mile in the customer's shoes.

Culture is not on paper. It's what people choose to do without being told. As the Harvard professors point out, indoctrination is important, but it can take many forms. One way is to bring on the kinds of challenges that can only be met by practicing what the company preaches.

Put your ideology to work by taking long shots, possible only with confidence bearing on arrogance. It's something you hear a lot these days. People are quoting Steve Jobs and pointing to Facebook office art that says *"Move Fast and Break Things."* Naturally, it's not going to say *Drag Your Feet and Cover Your Ass,* because everyone, even at Facebook, already knows to do that. But a word of caution is in order.

As an individual, I've taken plenty of risks: jobs I didn't know how to do, startups I knew very little about, plus the literal crazy-long shots on the basketball court. As a company, however, our biggest goal is to do good work and enjoy it. As much as we want to psych ourselves up and be bold, we are deeply, passionately and steadfastly against stress.

Can you have it both ways: risky, and stress-free? You figure it out. All I know is that, at my company, we like to start small and double- and triple-check every step. We set loose deadlines for software updates, like "sometime within the next month." And we do whatever the customer asks for—mostly small changes that add up to their culture, not ours.

Let's now take Mark Zuckerberg, just because there is so much stuff on him in the press. He is big on personal challenges. *Bloomberg Businessweek* says he invents a new one every year. In 2010 it was learning Mandarin. In 2011—to eat only the animals he slaughtered himself. And in 2013, it was to meet a new person each day.

But what kinds of goals has he set for Facebook? In a 2004 interview with CNBC, a few months after the launch, the twenty-year-old Zuckerberg said he had originally hoped for

400 or 500 users. At the time of the interview Facebook already had 100,000. Next goal? *"Who knows where we're going next …maybe we can make something cool!"*

This doesn't mean you don't make big plays when it's the right thing to do. Did you notice that 2012 was missing from Mark Zuckerberg's list of annual challenges? That's probably because in 2012 Facebook went mobile first. That was a huge shift he personally put into effect by shutting down any meeting that focused on computers rather than smartphones.

Those are my thoughts on *core ideology*, which the professors say takes you halfway to a "winning culture." The other half is *stimulating progress*, which is itself part of the core. They urge you to train your people to learn by trial and error; to look for improvements, try new things, and take small failures in stride.

STIMULATING PROGRESS—A HOW-TO

Only ten years ago, Facebook itself was a new thing, and there was nothing to do there, but to try and fail and try again. Now things look different, at least on the outside. The company has a billion users and lots of established practices that have earned record profits.

When not in survival mode, a company has to rely on culture to keep itself mobile, so to speak. That's why after a few years of wild success, Facebook so wisely decided to solidify its creative core. And by the way, if you don't think of culture as your company's creative core, you are still missing the point of all the far-out examples I've crammed into this book. Going out on a limb is like yoga for our creative brain, the one that allows us to see problems in a new light. If you want people to think new thoughts on your behalf, then, every now and again, let them feel like they can do no wrong.

What's outrageous in Facebook's case is the medium they've chosen to diffuse their inner branding. A company that has digitalized one billion lives is going hard copy to reach its own people. Ben Barry, Facebook's "minister of propaganda," and Everett Katigbak created their Analog Research Lab for that very purpose.

Analog Research Lab is just a funny name for a printing press. The real lab is Facebook employees, all of whom have a standing invitation to come create their own inspirational art completely uncensored. Barry teaches screen-printing classes on both coasts. He also invites artists-in-residence to come leave their mark on the company. The Lab has produced posters like *"Move fast and break things," "Likers Gonna Like,"* and *"What Would You Do If You Weren't Afraid?"* After Facebook had signed up its billionth user, a little red book appeared on every employee's desk. Its title: *Facebook was not originally created to be a company.*

And what does all of this do for Facebook? *"It makes it more collaborative,"* says Barry. *"People feel ownership. They get to see this stuff is made by hand, not spit out by a digital printer somewhere. And it gives them a much greater appreciation for all the stuff they see around them, which has been really awesome."*[35]

People feel ownership because they have ownership. *"I always laugh when people email me asking for permission to do stuff,"* Barry says. *"And I'm like, I'm not the gatekeeper on this, just do it!"*

If you read that last comment and said to yourself, "That's the kind of freedom you give people *after* you've already built a strong culture," you are not incorrect. Freedom and trust must grow with the culture, not ahead of it. The trick is to set your intention. Are you waiting for employees to become trustworthy before you defer to their judgment? Or, are you actively seeking ways to support and empower people *as they are*?

This subtle shift in the company's attitude, even unseen and unannounced, can be all the "starter" you need to grow your culture. Without it, none of the other ideas in this book will do you any good. And it's the first place to look when your efforts are being ungratefully thwarted.

Next step: just listen and observe. There is a common understanding among your people already. Things they all like and don't like. Things that speak to them and things that turn them off. Pick something small and make a friendly gesture by doing things *their* way. Here's a quick story.

The IT department at Beauty Co. had a time-honored tradition. Once a month all the rank and file would go out to lunch at a Chinese buffet. For $10 a head, we'd stuff our faces until every part of our anatomy not responsible for digesting food would shut down. Then we'd scrabble back to our desks and just sit there for the next hour not even pretending to be of any use. Everybody loved it. The management turned the blind eye—all except my boss. He'd go around and try to give us tasks, before disappearing into his office. To do what? Obviously the same thing we were trying to do: sit down and digest. None of us would have it. If he was going to sit his fat ass down, so would we. We'd hide in the empty offices and go to sleep, or march into the server room as a group and sit there.

While going for the world record in work ethic, the help-desk admiral missed out on a real chance to connect with his crew. His mistake is a common one, because most companies live not by one, but two sets of standards: the real one and the fake one.

The real culture is what you really like. The fake culture is the face the company puts on out of insecurity and lack of imagination. The two are naturally at odds, and much effort is wasted in asserting one against the other. The genius of Stratton Oakmont was to merge these two and release enough power to bring to life the most obscene fantasies of its generation.

The real culture often rises in response to the corporate put-on, or simply as a way to cope with the harsh demands of the business. It's like the immune system for your company. Don't fight it. Support it and use it to your advantage. The management at Beauty Co. could have scored major trust points by sponsoring our Chinese lunches. They could have also learned a lot of useful stuff had they cared to join us.

Most companies never close the gap between the real and the put-on. Forget companies. Most *people* are completely delusional about what they stand for, and that's assuming they are not boldface liars. But if you are interested, there is an easy way to tell whether your HR and your people live on the same planet. Stand by the water cooler. (If you are a virtual company like us, start a virtual "water cooler" social networking site on your intranet.) And listen. Do your employees refer to the company as *"we"* or *"they?"*

Moving from *"they"* to *"we"* is a big task, but it doesn't need to happen all at once. The remaining chapters are about breaking the ice and mending fences between you and your people on the enterprise scale. Loathsome company policies are always a great place to start. NetApp (no. 33 on *Fortune's* 2014 list and one-time top-spot holder) started many years ago by rewriting its elaborate travel policy. The new policy reads: *"We are a frugal company. But don't show up dog-tired to save a few bucks. Use your common sense."*

CHAPTER 17

START AT THE TOP

❝Your anger at the slightest imperfection in others is a sure sign that you have high standards. (Double standards, but high nonetheless.)❞

— SCOTT ADAMS, *The Joy of Work*

❝Be gentle and you can be bold; be frugal and you can be liberal; avoid putting yourself before others and you can become a leader among men.❞

— LAO TZU

Albert Schweitzer said, *"Example is leadership."* His contemporary, Mahatma Gandhi, had a similar widely publicized thought: *"Be the change you wish to see in the world."*

What about a change you wish to see in your company? How is that going?

If the company is slowly moving in the wrong direction, it's likely that the leadership is not practicing what it preaches. It's okay. It's easy for professional saints like Gandhi and Schweitzer to live by their word. The rest of us were born with a double standard, and getting rid of it is like passing a kidney stone. Shall we begin?

For many companies, *walking the talk* is the hardest task there is. That's because life doesn't often imitate PowerPoint. One's designed to make you look good, the other—to prove you wrong.

In the previous chapter we talked about choosing the real over the put-on for your company. This chapter is about choosing the real for yourself.

In the long run, being real is the only thing that works with people, so it's worth a shot. Why does it work? Check out this short blog post in *Psychology Today* by Nan Russell, "Trust: The New Workplace Currency" (July 28, 2013). She says, *"The problem in most workplaces is distrust, not disengagement ... If you want engagement, you need trust."*

Forget about employee engagement for a moment. Going after it directly is a little like asking people to contribute to your cause. And we all love being pressured and guilted into other people's agendas. Try creating trust first. Trust doesn't automatically make people want to work for you, but it makes it possible for them to focus on all the things that do, like goals, relationships, service, etc. And, according to Nan, Simon Sinek, and others, trust is the most commonly missing ingredient.

Companies have countless opportunities to make it hard for people to trust them. Most prominent of these are usually actions (or non-actions) of senior leaders. Such was the case with Beauty Co., the establishment that inspired me to search for a better way to work.

At the helm of Beauty Co. was "Hermit Crab," the third generation chairman and CEO of Crabco, Beauty Co.'s parent company. According to Mr. Crab, Beauty Co. was rooted in such Crab family values as integrity, commitment, and customer service. I can't speak for the family, since they were rarely around to showcase their values. As for those employees who actually did show up for work, we had no idea what he was talking about.

The truth was Herm never met most of us. He never talked to us. No attempt to contact him ever made it past his overzealous secretary. So how would he know our values? But guess who did? Someone who walked around the office every day, running phony software upgrades and fixing computers! After a few months at the IT help desk, I knew exactly what was on people's minds. All I had to do was to look at the screen window they clumsily tried to hide when I came up behind them.

People at the corporate offices of Beauty Co. and its affiliated ventures didn't like to work. So there goes integrity and commitment. Our core values actually looked more like this:

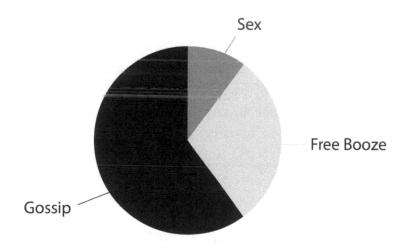

Twice a year, Crabco put on a tradeshow. All the hairdressers from nearby towns came to try out new products and have a little family fun. The IT Dept. was always in full attendance. Our official purpose was to set up point-of-sale computers.

The opening night featured Top 40 dance hits and open bar. The hairdressers got smashed and flocked to the dance floor. This was the moment we'd been waiting for the entire year. All the office people would join in, with management cheering on the wallflowers and the newbies.

By the end of the night, everyone hooked up with everyone— age, rank and marital status notwithstanding. At my first tradeshow, a VP of sales, fourteen years my senior, practically dragged me into her room. She was so hung over the next day that she skipped the rest of the show. Everyone knew about it, and you'd wonder how she even kept her job. Thanks to an unwritten code of silence, whatever happened at a tradeshow, stayed at the tradeshow.

Everyone loved the tradeshows, except Herm, who would not be caught dead fraternizing with employees. Except for one particular employee. He was dating a C-level secretary from one of the sister companies. The consensus was that she was in it for his money. Herm was twice her age and three times her size.

Was Herm guilty of misusing his post? In my opinion, yes … but not because he took interest in a young, attractive and possibly married employee. It's rather what he didn't do that bothers me. If you are the CEO and people gossip about you no matter what, you might as well use your star power to model a behavior you want in your company. He could have made a big difference with minimal effort. All he had to do was … use his computer.

In 2001, Beauty Co. was one of the most technology-resistant companies in the Western Hemisphere. It was full of people behaving as though their PCs had communicable diseases. (Which some of them probably did, given the things I found inside.) I was curious why management didn't do something about it—until I met the CEO.

Herm's office was usually empty and looked uninhabited, except maybe for the ghost of his predecessor. One day, when I came in to run a security patch on his PC, he was actually in, and we had a conversation.

> TIM: Hi, Mr. Crab. I need to update your computer.
> HERMIT CRAB: Oh, hi there. I have a question for you. How do I put my password into Outlook?
> TIM: You click on the Outlook icon, and when the password box comes up, you type it in.
> HERMIT CRAB: What is my password?
> TIM: Here, I reset it to "whatismypassword," all lower case.
> HERMIT CRAB: Where are my emails?
> TIM: You deleted them, and they are in your trash folder ...

Fast-forward fourteen years. Although these days I get a different set of questions, the root of the problem remains. People still shy away from the unfamiliar. Consequently, a perennial Biggest Challenge at Work is, "How do I get people to use new technology?"

Job Title	Biggest Challenge at Work
Manager, Order Services	*"Technology & resistance to change"*
IT Director	*"That my employees are intentionally dense with technology"*

If this is your issue, watch how your top execs interact with the piece of technology you are trying to promote. Chances are they are just as intentionally dense as the little guys. Train the execs first—or, at the very least, their almighty assistants. If the visible people around the office don't make the change, neither will the gray masses.

We have just discussed the no. 1 Cardinal Sin of Leadership: being fake and remote. It obviously won't help your employees reach for the stars. But it does help you avoid CSL no. 2: manic narcissism in the name of setting yourself as a shining example for people to follow.

This story takes us inside the ambitious young mind of CEO "Johnny Bologna" and his company, BolognaWorks, LLC. Like the CEO of Beauty Co., Johnny had neither built his company, nor worked his way through the ranks. He simply inherited his title from his father. *"Growing up, I knew I wanted to be a CEO,"* he writes in his blog post, *What Does a CEO Do?*

Young Steve Jobs wanted to make some money so he wouldn't have to sleep on the floor and walk seven miles for a meal. Young Mark Zuckerberg wanted to make something cool. For them, being a CEO was a means to an end. Johnny is different. He is a CEO who needs something to do. Like what?

To formulate his purpose, Johnny studies world leaders and famous CEOs. After years of research and contemplation, he is ready to reveal his vision to his employees. It looks something like this:

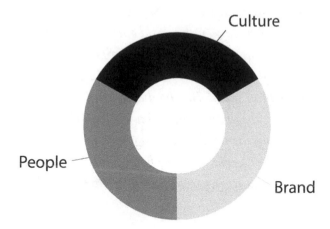

The employees (at least certain ones) can't contain their enthusiasm.

> *"Great advice for all aspiring leaders!"*
>
> *"Fantastic, looking forward to the next one."*
>
> *"Fantastic read! It's really important for companies to get that it's more than just product. You've nailed this one perfectly, Johnny! Bravo!"*

And finally, the grand prize winner. The one that leaves all the amateur ass-kissers in the dust:

> *Like Martin Luther King, John Fitzgerald Kennedy and Nelson Mandela before him, Johnny Bologna shows the true wisdom, humility and leadership*

qualities necessary to turn this world around for the better. To those men the world once said it couldn't be done, but they did it. To Jesus of Nazareth they once said, "No. It can't be done. You can't turn water into wine." But he did it. And to Johnny Bologna they have said, "You can't do that. You can't singlehandedly stand against all odds and change the world."... but he is doing it. And the world is watching with anticipation to see what he does next.

Are you embarrassed yet, Johnny?

Not at all.

Next comes a series of all-hands meetings featuring Johnny on stage wearing a headset and quoting himself on a huge screen in front of a suspiciously quiet audience. The meeting is an excuse for Johnny to praise himself for such epic achievements as: (a) Transforming the boardroom from green walls, maple table, and yellow chairs, to black walls, white table and black chairs. The COO, who happens to be Johnny's first cousin Mikey, is on hand to confirm that the new color scheme boosts his creativity; (b) Taking down the cubicle partitions; and (c) Making videos of people wearing horses' heads and dancing to happy music.

Throughout the talk, Johnny refers to himself as "we, your leaders." He calls his initiatives "brilliant" and the results "beautiful." The people also get praise—for "doing a great job embracing." Embracing or not, they are now called Godfather of IT, Wizards of Wow, Warriors of Wow (one's sales, the other customer service) and other such nonsense.

After hogging the stage for half an hour, Johnny lets his HR rep who, by the way, goes by Happiness Relations, have the spotlight. She actually has some numbers to report: she's hired fifteen new warriors and wizards. And just when I have my first glimpse of hope that there's some sanity left in the company, she delivers a crushing blow. Earth Day is coming up, she says, and the company has big plans. Half of the people will celebrate by sitting in the dark and the other half will not be using the printers—to reduce BolognaWorks' carbon footprint. The shocking part is that no one's laughing. They must all know that the Happiness enforcer is dead serious.

The path of leadership is wrought with many pitfalls. People like Johnny and Hermit, who received it as a birthright, may be more vulnerable than those that earned their stripes. But we are all liable to make gigantic horses' asses of ourselves. Hats off to Johnny for knowingly or unknowingly taking that risk. After all, he only obeyed the battle cry of his generation: speak your mind and follow your heart. Unfortunately, it's not until after we've followed through that we find out whether our minds and hearts are solid gold.

Oops. Now what?

Take it from Martha Stewart. The best thing to do when you take a wrong turn is to quickly admit your mistake and change course. In 2004, Martha was convicted of insider trading and went to a federal prison. Many people thought the prison sentence would end her public career. They were wrong. Upon her release in March 2005, Martha made a full and spectacular comeback in business, on television and in live appearances all over the world. I saw Martha in Boston in late 2014. Her housewifely spreads won't fool me again. In business dealings, she is about as soft and feminine as a sledgehammer. But she knows something about leadership: there is no moving forward without owning your shit first.

Prancing around on stage and plastering your face all over the website is not leadership. Taking responsibility is, and it means sacrificing your pride, not pumping your ego. It also means showing trust in people, not demanding it of them. These are the best examples you can set for your employees. Imagine if everyone in the company could easily say, "My bad, let me fix it." Imagine if everyone in the company could trust everyone else to have his back when things don't go according to plan.

Two real-life examples of this before we move on.

Neil Davidson and Simon Galbraith, the founders of highly successful Redgate, made their share of mistakes. They said so right on their website. Until recently, you could read this story on Redgate's About page:

> ... *we blew every opportunity we had. We blew those opportunities because of our inexperience, myopia, and confusion. Because we'd been blinded by our early financial success. We were chumps. [...] We knew very little about the market, about what our customers needed, about who they were, and how we could help them ...*

They could have spun the same story as one of heroic effort crowned by roaring success. But they chose to send a different message. It says that Redgate is *about* taking responsibility, not tooting its own horn.

The second example is about trust. Statistical software company SAS is famous for two things: profitability and generosity towards employees. In January of 2009, after sales had plummeted and many of the competitors announced layoffs, SAS founder and CEO Jim Goodnight told employees the company would not cut any of its 13,000 jobs around the world. Instead, he simply asked the people to watch their spending and help the company survive the crisis. They did better than survive. SAS posted record profits during the financial crisis of 2008–09, just as they had done every year since inception. He later said, *"By making it very clear that no one was going to be laid off, suddenly we cut out huge amounts of chatter, concern, and worry—and people got back to work."*[36]

Simon Sinek says that's actually how leadership works. People are willing to let you have your stock options, your corner office, and, if you must, even your DD-sized assistant—for a price—so you cover for them when disaster strikes. You do it first, without asking: why should I? He says, leaders don't sacrifice people for the sake of numbers. You put people first, and they will get you the numbers. And he gets a standing ovation every time.

If you've ever started a company, you don't need Sinek to lecture you on eating last. You literally get paid last or not at all. But even when your company is stable and there is plenty of money to go around, the responsibility doesn't end.

Speaking for Axero, Vivek and I chose to give our employees total freedom. The flip side of that is that we are left to pick up all the slack. For instance: (1) We are always available. Axero has no face-time policy. We are 100 percent remote and everyone works a different set of hours. That means people should be able to reach me anytime of the day or night, if they need to. I just have to trust them not to call me at 3:00 in the morning unless it's really urgent. (2) We are present. Anyone in a leadership position has to stay in contact with the people. Share content. Start discussions. Answer questions. (3) We do mundane work. Like customer support—even when we have enough people to cover the phones. Because if they see me doing it, they know it's important. (4) We work the most hours in the company. No 4-hour workweek here.

If you do leadership right, you may get the cult following advocated by the authors of *Built to Last*. But don't lust after it. Don't try to force it with copy-paste tactics. And whatever you do, don't substitute hype for a real contribution to people's lives. Don't put words in their mouths and don't try to fill their heads with propaganda.

Shallow enthusiasm may turn people off faster than it sucks them in. Here's one of the answers to *What is the worst part about working at Google?* on Quora:

> *The worst part of working for Google is the people. In order to get in to work at Google you have to be the kind of person who "whoops" when your CEO comes in the conference room. And screams with excitement when they announce "We've introduced … searching by pictures!!!"*

DON'T CONFUSE CULT AND CULTURE

You don't need to draw attention to your own person to stay true to yourself and do great things. Before passing away, Steve Jobs told Tim Cook, his handpicked successor, to never ask himself, *"What would Steve Jobs do?"*[37] Steve's final advice is well heeded.

Tim Cook is taking steps that would have never made it past Steve, like buying back shares, making peace with Google, and treating people with respect. At the same time, Tim's personality remains in the shadow of his legendary predecessor. In some ways it's as if Steve had never left.

> *He is in my heart. He is deep in Apple's* DNA. *His spirit will always be the foundation of the company. I literally think about him every day. His office is still left as it was. His name is still on the door …*[38]

Here's another case of a humble, yet effective way of leading by example. You've probably never heard of this guy, but he's taken his company to no. 17 on *Fortune's* "100 Best Companies to Work For" in 2014, and not just that.

General Joe Robles, Jr., became CEO of USAA in 2007. Since then, the insurance company, which had been around for nearly a century, has grown 53 percent in membership, 45 percent in revenue, and 68 percent in net worth. This is despite the financial crisis of 2008–09 and some of the highest catastrophe losses in history. It's won the top financial strength ratings from every insurance-rating agency in the U.S. And it gets all kinds of recognition for its customer service.

How does he do it? General Joe heavily invests in culture. He calls himself *Chief Culture Officer* and constantly works with consultants to spit-shine his people, starting with himself. You can find him on *Fast Company's* "30-second MBA" videos. This is what he believes works for him and what he models for others:

- **Communicate, communicate, communicate.** If 100 percent of the people hear the message ten times, they will deliver on it. The mission statement is especially important.

- **Listen.** When faced with a challenge, ask many people at all levels in the company what they think. If still undecided, find a mentor, someone who has the experience you lack.
- **Read.** Change is the only constant. Read as much as you can about what works in your industry and life in general.

This is excellent advice, but there is something else. People who built great companies didn't do it for the same reasons for which they are praised afterwards. In other words, things never look the same in retrospect, as they did looking forward.

Books are written in retrospect. Words like *brand* and *culture* were coined by scholars to describe things that happened in the past to other people. You can benefit from their insights, as I have, but you also have to live your own life going forward. Not someone else's life going back.

Find what moves you. Much of this book is about how to motivate other people. This chapter is about you. The deeper your sense of purpose, the more you will be able to win people to your cause. Johnny Bologna is not the only one who craves his family's approval and hordes of screaming fans. We all do. Look beyond that. What do you see?

CHAPTER 18
COMMUNICATE

❝ Number one, cash is king ... number two, communicate ...
number three, buy or bury the competition. **❞**
— JACK WELCH

❝ Quote me as saying I was mis-quoted. **❞**
— GROUCHO MARX

In 2014 About.com took an online poll to find out why people
don't care for their jobs. The top three causes, together accounting
for 62 percent of all responses, were all communication related:

Lack of direction from management: 38 percent
Poor communication overall: 13 percent
Constant change that's not well-communicated: 11 percent[39]

Constant change is understandably tough to communicate. New
things confuse people, especially when they come at a rapid pace.
But what about those timeless principles Collins and Porras
advocate in *Built to Last?* Do employees at least know what their
companies have always stood for?

In 2013 TINYpulse surveyed 40,000 employees from 300
companies around the globe. Only 42 percent of them knew

their employer's vision, mission, and values. The study concluded that *"too many executives are not communicating and reinforcing their company's guiding principles and mission."*[40]

General Joe Robles would likely agree with such a conclusion. And it is his top priority to not become one of these executives. Notice too that he is not simply repeating a mission statement every chance he gets. He is building a culture where the mission is accepted and understood. This is why he is the Chief Culture Officer. And this is why we will not be talking about the company mission until Chapter 21. Before we get to that, there are a few fundamentals we need to cover.

This book is about how employees relate to their employers and their jobs. Is it *we* or *they*? Are we standing on common ground or a battlefield? Whether managers succeed or fail as leaders ultimately depends on these attitudes. So, let's see how our communication *creates* them. This is important. Let's not assume that people will do whatever they do regardless of what you say. Let's take a fresh look at what actually happens to individuals, relationships, and culture around us when we open and shut our mouths.

But first, a quick parable: I am a visual guy, and this one really helps me focus before I open my mouth and make a stinking mess. It's been around for a while, so you may have heard it before. Even so, do me a favor and give it your full attention. It just may change the way you talk to people and, consequently, the way people talk and listen to you. If I had read it in a book, I may have let it in one ear and out the other. The reason it stuck with me has something to do with how I learned it.

I have a very successful friend. A few years ago he dropped off the face of the Earth. I thought I had lost him forever, but two years later, he called me out of the clear blue sky. He eventually confessed that he had been battling addiction and depression. At his lowest point, he woke up in a hospital having no memory of how he got there. He told me he was back on his feet, and he was never going to let it happen to him again. I was curious what made him so sure. That's when he told me the parable. It goes something like this:

> *"Grandfather, why do people fight?" a Cherokee child asks his chief. "Well" the old man replies, "we all have two wolves inside us: a white wolf and a gray wolf. The gray wolf is filled with fear, anger, envy, jealousy, greed, and arrogance. The white wolf is filled with peace, love, hope, courage, humility, compassion, and faith. They battle constantly." The chief pauses. And the child asks impatiently: "But grandfather, which wolf wins?" "The one that we feed," says the old man.*

"I let the gray wolf out," said my friend. "That's when all the shit happened. I know he'll always be there. He's never going to leave. But now I can see him rearing his head and I turn the other way."

The wolves are our attitudes. We have to assume that we are ultimately free to choose one over the other, otherwise what's the point of self-help? But we can make it easier or harder on ourselves and others to choose right. We feed the wolves by our thoughts, words, and actions, all of which add up to the way we communicate.

Before we go any further, let's agree that we are looking for white wolf to white wolf communication. And let's be clear what that is. What colors your words is your intention, not the actual words you use. I am not an angry person, but I swear often. It actually puts people at ease. It sounds bizarre, but trust me, the moment your employees relax enough to curse in front of you is a magical one.

At the other extreme, if you fill the air at your company with nicey-nice propaganda, your real intention is to dominate your people, not to empower them. No matter how hard you choose your words, you will always rub people the wrong way. Even if they don't openly fight you, they will silently resist you. They will think non-conformist thoughts and whisper behind your back. That's disengagement. And it's gray wolf to gray wolf.

"Fine," you say, "I can be responsible for my end. But what if I do it right, and they still take it the wrong way?"

Well, anyone can be responsible for his end. If you are in the business of leadership, management, or what our friend Johnny Bologna calls Happiness Relations, you need to be responsible for the whole cycle: what you say, what they hear, and what they understand and make up in their heads.

I hope some of you are nodding your heads vigorously at this point and saying, "two-way communication." Consider that communication within your company actually happens in three ways: (1) company to employees; (2) employees to company; and (3) employees to employees and other people, including potential employees ... and that all three of these start with what you say or don't say.

And here's the takeaway ...

> *Your whole power to pull together, lead, and transform your company hinges on your ability to influence these three streams of communication.*

Let's take them one at a time.

COMPANY-TO-EMPLOYEES

The most important way a company talks to employees is through the actions of its leaders. That's what I said in Chapter 17, *Start at the Top*, and it's still true in this chapter.

Acting out our principles is about all the evangelizing we do at Axero. Vivek and I don't sit around and define our culture for the future generations of Axeroids. We don't ask what working for Axero means to people, or how we can all have a bigger impact on humanity. We just take care of our direct business and our people day-by-day, and everyone kind of gets it for the most part.

I hear it doesn't work like that in big companies. In a huge company, the right message at the top can get scrambled on its way down. You know that game where the teacher sits all the kids in a row and whispers something into the first child's ear. The first child turns to the second child and whispers it to him, and so on, and so on, until the end of the row. The last child gets up and says out loud what he'd heard … and everybody laughs because it's not what the teacher said or what other kids passed along.

Something similar happens in companies, not only because people don't get the right message, but also because people tend to do what's easy as opposed to what's right, even when they know what that is. This book should help you make what's right also easy to do. However, there are always these very basic things, like taking criticism, admitting a mistake, or making a change, that don't sit well with people. We are all fallible just by virtue of being human. That makes reaching your audience a far greater task than crafting the right message.

When asked about an opening night of one of his plays, George Bernard Shaw famously replied, *"The play was a great success, but audience was a dismal failure."* Failing their internal audiences is something companies do frequently and almost by default. Here are some of the typical gripes I get in response to my Biggest Challenge at Work quiz:

Job Title	Biggest Challenge at Work
Director, Communications	*"Reaching employees who are not online"*
Ultrasound Supervisor	*"Communication"*
Operations/IT Manager	*"How our processes are linked"*
Sales Manager	*"Timely communications"*
Consultant	*"Understanding"*
Executive Director	*"My board doesn't recognize the hard work of my employees"*

What can companies do to make sure that people listen, hear, understand, and take action? First off, assume numerous and unexpected barriers to communication. The more people and layers in the organization, the harder you have to work to get your point across. Speak to people whenever the moment seems right, as well as at regular intervals. Use any means appropriate to the occasion. Don't just tell people what to do. Give them a clear line-of-sight: where they are going, how they are doing, and where each one fits in. Promptly address concerns.

Remember, the problem is not just on their end. Every time you talk to people, you make assumptions about them. You do this automatically, without thinking, and your assumptions are mostly wrong. This is a fact that has been proven in many experiments. There is almost no one who is so enlightened and self-aware that he never makes this mistake. What happens when you misjudge people? They get offended. They actively or passive-aggressively resist you—and you blame them, not knowing that you, yourself, have caused their resistance.

What to do? First off, don't worry about being wrong. If you don't show your wrongness, how will it get corrected? I know, I know, you'd rather figure it out on your own. But you can't count on being right all the time, can you? So, give yourself room to be wrong, and don't defend yourself in hindsight. Defensiveness is the number one enemy of communication. Instead, learn to communicate in ways that appeal to people's humanity. Expect to make public mistakes and use them to cure yourself and your whole company of being defensive.

EMPLOYEES-TO-COMPANY

In *Leadership Skills for Managers* George Bernard Shaw said that "The single biggest problem in communication is the illusion that it has taken place." What did he mean by that? Very simply, communication is not issuing a statement. Nor is it receiving a response. Communication, the kind that matters, is reaching common ground. At the very minimum, both sides need to feel that they have been heard.

Companies have long been trying to get employees to listen. The recent rise of social intranets is yet another attempt. Unlike the standard static variety, the social intranet lets people talk back. Even that, for many of our clients, isn't good enough. Can we require people to comment when we post news, Tim? How can we make sure they read it? Do you have a button that says: I've read this? Do we get notified if someone hasn't? And can we please turn off private messaging? We want to see what people are saying!

So far, so good. We have you covered. But what about all the things employees need to get off their chests? How can companies get in on what matters to people?

In Chapter 19, *Give Them a Voice*, we will talk about all the different ways a company can hear from employees. For now, let's just agree that it needs to happen. If people are to feel ownership and empowerment in their jobs, they need to be able to tell their side of the story. And, just like the companies, people need more than an outlet to speak their minds. They need to feel heard.

EMPLOYEES-TO-EMPLOYEES AND OTHER PEOPLE

The ultimate test of your communication is what people say to each other when you are not there. Is your point of view still present? Does it make a difference? Does it serve your purpose?

This is where it helps to be straightforward. If you leave room for interpretation, interpretation is what you'll get—around and outside the office. Wherever your people talk to families, friends, coworkers, competitors, and sympathetic strangers, there will be rumors, gossip, suspicion, and resentment. Especially if the news is bad.

I am going to tell you a story about giving bad news. It deals with something companies do a lot—firing people. Firing is communication. It tells people what the company really stands for and what to expect of it in the near future. And everybody listens.

For most people, being fired is a major life event, like, say, a divorce. Not only do all of their friends and family want to know what happened, but the employee himself wants to make sense of things and tell his story. So you have an emotional and highly "engaged" storyteller on one hand—and an eager audience on the other. Do you hope to convert your employees into your "brand ambassadors"? Do you have social media buttons on your company blog, just in case it happens? I do too. However, a more likely source of the inside scoop on your company are the former employees answering the inevitable question, "What happened?" And it doesn't have to be bad. Here's how it's worked for my buddy Brian.

Brian is a professional musician. He plays in a band and is also the band's sole owner. He pays people to play with him during his live shows. Brian's band travels a lot. They don't just play together. They eat, sleep, and take bathroom breaks together. The other day he called me to ask how to fire someone without inviting drama. He was talking about a trumpet player he had hired a few weeks earlier. The guy just didn't get "together." "Pull over the van, I need to get a granola bar." "Drop me off at the gym, I need to work out." Brian frequently opens for other bands, and his players stick around till after the concert to network with the headliner. All but the trumpet, who had better things to do and left immediately after the opening act. Brian's mind was made up.

Before calling me, Brian had asked his father's opinion. Brian's dad had owned all sorts of businesses and done well at all of them. Dad stood on his rights: "You don't owe him a reason, just get rid of him." I wasn't so sure. What kind of a feeling do you want to create between yourself and the guy? People deserve to be treated with respect, especially when they can badmouth you after you fire them. Respect doesn't mean giving up your position. You can make it clear that it's over, but give exact reasons why. Don't leave it up to him to make up his own reasons. "We stick around after the show. You don't. That doesn't work for us." Case closed.

Brian agreed with me. Later he called to say that he'd had the talk. Surprisingly, it was the first time the two of them saw eye to eye. The trumpet said, "Yeah, I saw it coming. It wasn't working for me, either." Instead of creating hard feelings, the firing actually resolved them. Something to think about!

My point here is that you can make any bad news worse by how you deliver it. You may think that there's nothing you can do about the way people react to the news. But, in reality, people are reacting to you, and you can do a lot to spare their dignity, no matter what the news. Don't make it all their fault and their problem. Give up the blame. Own your share of the consequences. And watch what happens.

PUTTING IT ALL TOGETHER

In a 2013 white paper, *A New Way to Work*, Unify (formerly Siemens Enterprise Communications) offered these tips to companies looking to engage employees: (a) Tell people what they need to know to do their jobs well; (b) Use internal and external social networks; (c) Listen as you speak: start and join multi-way conversations; (d) Access all media types, information, and people; (e) Respond in real-time; (f) Aggregate networks; (g) Add intelligence to filter, summarize, and act on events; (h) Use plain language.

If you're serious about doing all of that, you'll need software that allows you to have real-time conversations that involve everyone on your team.

Ultimately your company is about building knowledge. Can you do it through email?

Let's say someone in your company solves a problem for a customer through email. How many people know about that? Things get lost easily in the inbox, and when other people can't see them, they get lost forever. What happens to a short lifetime's worth of email when an employee leaves the company? If the company uses a third party carrier, like Gmail, he takes it home with him. Else—it ingloriously perishes in the great Corporate Inbox.

Email is not a good way to extract or preserve knowledge—or connect teams. If you want a quick fix to productivity and engagement, don't just tell people to break the silos. Get yourself into a collaborative space where you can have conversations and search for answers. You'll be shocked at how much process improvement happens automatically.

Finally, does it matter what words you use, as long as you get your point across? Well, if you want people to read *and* comment on your posts, it helps if you don't make their eyes glaze over the page. Eradicate business jargon. Keep it plain.

Thomas J. Watson, Jr., IBM's second and most powerful CEO, had no patience for corporate speak. Tom Jr. succeeded his father as CEO of IBM in 1956. He is still one of the best examples of how to talk to employees. In 1970, he made this passionate appeal:

> *A foreign language has been creeping into many of the presentations I hear and the memos I read. It adds nothing to a message but noise, and I want your help in stamping it out. It's called gobbledygook.*

There's no shortage of examples. Nothing seems to get finished anymore it gets "finalized." Things don't happen at the same time but "coincident with this action." Believe it or not, people will talk about taking a "commitment position" and then because of the "volatility of schedule changes" they will "decommit" so that our "posture vis-à-vis some data base that needs a sizing will be able to enhance competitive positions." That's gobbledygook.

Gone wrong, communication is a festering sore. Done right, it's a miracle cure. If you want people to do their best work for you, how you talk to them makes a big difference. And, since communication done right is 80 percent listening and 20 percent talking, how you listen is even more important than how you talk.

So, how *do* you listen to your employees?

CHAPTER 19
GIVE THEM A VOICE

❝Somewhere in a vast wasteland of cubicles, copiers, and conference rooms, an idea is about to be born. It is just a soul of an idea, twinkling in and out of existence, waiting for the right combination of matter and energy to provide form and motion … In time, with the right combination of hope and dreams and risk, the idea can become large enough to change the world.❞

— SCOTT ADAMS, *The Joy of Work*

In 1988, *Inc.* published an article under the headline, "I'm Sorry, Yvon's out Surfing—How to run a company when you're gone six months of the year." The article is about how Yvon Chouinard, the founder of Patagonia, runs his company without sacrificing his life's passion—the great outdoors.

How?

The article briefly mentions something called the 5-15 report, a piece of paper all Patagonia employees filled out and all managers read—weekly. Each report only took fifteen minutes to write and five minutes to read. In addition, managers compiled summaries of their subordinates' reports for their managers, and so on, until a filtered and synthesized version of the report reached the CEO, wherever he happened to be at the moment.

A more recent article by management columnist Harvey Schachter shows the contents of a 5-15 report, which since then has become a popular management tool:

5-15 REPORT

- **Name:**

- **Week ending:**

- **Accomplishments for the week:**
  (List completed activities and notable accomplishments. In general, what is working? What is your current situation?)

- **Priorities for next week:**
  (Be specific.)

- **Challenges/Roadblocks:**
  (Describe potential challenges that may impede your intended tasks/goals.)

- **Lessons Learned/Opportunities for Improvement:**
  (List any area that might benefit from improvement; questions you are trying to solve; lessons recently learned or relearned.)

Notice how this report and the protocol that accompanies it keeps not just the CEO, but everyone in the company in the loop. How it zeroes in on current and potential problems, but also on successful solutions. How it asks for creative input, but keeps it in the context of one's direct responsibilities.

Job Title	Biggest Challenge at Work
General Manager	*"Getting people to speak up"*

If you are like the guy who left the above comment, the 5-15 report is a great place to start. It's an easy, non-confrontational way for people to contribute their opinions from the privacy and comfort of their cubicles.

However, if you are out to build a company that functions like a single healthy organism and produces extraordinary output, then public debate may be the way to go. More and more CEOs train their people to disagree, and to do so in an open forum where everyone can have an immediate reaction.

Why do that? That was the question LinkedIn's Daniel Roth asked Carlos Ghosn, the man responsible for turning around not one but three car companies, all at the same time. Ghosn is the double CEO of the French automaker Renault and Japanese Nissan. He is also the chairman of AvtoVaz in Russia.

"You want debate," he says, *"very simply because you want to make good decisions."*

Challenging authority—or majority—is part of culture. Some teams, companies, or whole countries do it as a matter of course. Others put their trust in the judgments of their superiors. For Ghosn, that's just too bad. You never know if an idea has any merit until it's been thoroughly debated and either refined, rejected, or taken into a whole new direction.

He's managed inside what he calls *disciplined* cultures, where people are used to carrying out orders whether they agree with them or not. He puts Germans, Koreans, and Japanese into this category. He says it's absolutely critical to make these people debate pros and cons before setting plans in motion. Otherwise your bad idea will be executed with disastrous precision and speed.

He says it's equally important to have a public debate in cultures where people prefer to complain after the fact, like his native Latin America. This way everyone has had a chance to disagree and gauge the popularity of his own view. Knowing that they've been heard makes it easier for people to move forward once a decision is reached.

At the same time, the point of discussion is to make good decisions, not to satisfy every ego. So the method is important. Ghosn's idea is to have …

> *a very clear process by which you have a very formal forums where people debate questions and there are presentations about the pros and cons of different options and you allow the competent people to express themselves and the people who have something to say to express themselves.*[41]

Another company who always wants to hear from employees is Google. *"We try to have as many channels for expression as we can, recognizing that different people—and different ideas—will percolate up in different ways,"* says Laszlo Bock, Google's SVP of People Operations. In addition to talking to people face-to-face and on Google+, Google employs an intricate system of surveys to extract detailed feedback.

Asking for feedback saddles you with a responsibility: what will you do with it? Google, for one, believes it's just as important to empower people to find solutions as it is to encourage them to speak up about problems. Google's largest employee survey,

Googlegeist, covers hundreds of issues. Once the results are in, employees volunteer to solve the biggest problems, and management backs up their choice. This is how an engineering-to-product-management job rotation program came about. Another outcome is a company-wide pay raise. On top of *Googlegeist* and a host of other surveys, Google routinely reviews GUTS (Google Universal Ticketing Systems)—a place for employees to raise concerns about anything, similar to New York City's 311 line. An urgent case may call for a *FixIt*, a 24-hour stretch when the entire company focuses on solving a specific problem.

Yes, Google is a rich company, and they can afford this, among other employee perks and bizarre HR experiments. How about a nice conservative company at a time of financial crisis?

Edwards Jones proudly sits at no. 4 on *Fortune's* "100 Best Companies to Work For" in 2014. It's the fourth largest financial advisory firm in the U.S. The number of its locations rivals Starbucks. At the end of 2008 revenues fell, and the company was looking to save $100 million in costs to avoid losses. Instead of cutting jobs, Edward Jones turned to associates for cost-saving ideas. Management picked the best ideas and rewarded the winners with tickets to the MLB All Star Game in St. Louis. When the results were tallied, Edward Jones saved $120 million—plus the jobs and commitment of its people.

Is there a downside to openly discussing problems and solutions with employees? Google's Laszlo Bock believes it's a matter of managerial skill:

> *Some people will argue that giving employees so much information and such a loud voice leads to anarchy ... The reality is that every issue needs a*

*decision maker. Managed properly, the result of
these approaches is not some transcendent moment
of unanimity. Rather, it is a robust, data-driven
discussion that brings the best ideas to light, so
that when a decision is made it leaves the dissent-
ers with enough context to understand and respect
the rationale for the decision, even if they disagree
with the outcome.*[42]

ASK THEM WHAT THEY THINK

If you want your people to fully engage in their work, leave room
for their own voice and initiative. Never assume you know what
your employees think—let them tell you. Let them take part in
decision making. Be open to new ideas. Support employee-led
programs. In the words of Laszlo Bock,

> *People look for meaning in their work. People want
> to know what's happening in their environment.
> People want to have some ability to shape that
> environment.*

In 2003, IBM decided to rewrite its corporate values. Then
it did something strange—asking 50,000 employees what they
valued about their work. After three days of online discussions,
IBM ran all the comments through a text analyzer (eClassifier)
to look for themes. They learned that employees valued *"dedication to every client's success," "innovation that matters—for our
company and for the world,"* and *"trust and personal responsibility
in all relationships."* In 2004, IBM hosted another all-hands online

forum to find ways to act on those values. This time 52,000 employees brainstormed for seventy-two hours.

You cannot lead people without knowing what's on their minds any more than you can drive a car without knowing the function of the pedals, the transmission, and the steering wheel.

Employee surveys are a popular way to get feedback. Many vendors out there can't wait to sell you a survey—but be careful! There are a million questions you could ask. Choose the topics that make or break your company's spirit. SAS, for example, focuses on open communication, respect from fellow employees, transparency into career paths, and being treated as a human being.

As an executive, you want information that helps you make decisions. You want the bottom line. Sometimes you'll hear advice like "measure engagement." "If you can measure it, you can manage it," and so on. It may sound like a great idea. Why mess around with all these survey questions when, in the end, you can't even tell how you are doing? On the other hand, if you could put your finger on some solid stats, you could say something like this at your next staff meeting:

"Ladies and Gentlemen, thanks to our outstanding employee recognition programs, employee engagement is up to 70 percent this year. That's 20 percentage points higher than last year and 45 percentage points higher than the industry as a whole."

And then you'd get a standing ovation.

Do you really want to sound like that? Maybe you do. After all, expending massive man-hours to convert complex information into a number is better than completely ignoring the issue. Or is it? Some of these measuring schemes are a form of avoidance, actively promoted by Big Data.

Take sentiment analyzers, for example. This type of software works by extracting keywords from your company's message boards and comparing them to a set vocabulary to give you a number. Here's a vendor pitching it to potential customers who would like to keep their finger on their people's pulse:

> *Measuring sentiment presents an extremely complex task. For administrators, it's impossible to extract every message and score sentiment and emotion. It could take weeks or even months to aggregate the scores and gain insights into your organization. Luckily, there are text and sentiment software solutions that make this task much more manageable ...*[43]

Imagine the possibilities! An HR rep can now understand exactly how people feel about the company without ever leaving her cubicle. A lucky break, indeed!

Nevertheless, people like new bells and whistles. Who knows, maybe a plug-in sentiment analyzer would boost Communifire's entertainment value? Or maybe a VP of HR somewhere desperately wanted this feature. I was curious how much it cost. They said I had to be willing to spend at least $100,000 for the sales rep to return my call.

Please don't measure engagement or sentiment. If you have $100K burning a hole in your pocket, spend it on something that makes people happy. Save yourself the time it takes to analyze the charts and spend it with your people. You already have a free app for taking in sentiment. It's called your heart.

When things get too geeky and complicated, it's time to go back to basics. Listening to employees can be as simple as asking a few questions face-to-face. The Institute for Corporate Productivity (i4cp) recommends stay interviews—an alternative to exit interviews—to prevent unwanted turnover. Stay interviews help resolve minor issues and make employees feel valued.

Measuring success is important, but find something worth measuring. Like closed complaints, happy customers, profitability and growth. If you've invested into collaboration software, monitor high-level stats to make sure it's being used as intended. Use it yourself. You'll know what people are saying without relying on numbers. When it comes to human interaction, numbers can hide more than they reveal. Even when measured correctly, sentiment is only a symptom. Stay in conversation and go to the root of the problem. Don't get sidetracked by a number.

Just in case you are wondering if Axero uses surveys and stay interviews—we don't. We are a small company. Everyone talks to everyone. People don't put up a false front and don't hold back their questions and ideas. We tell people the minute we hire them: we want your feedback. Especially when you have a problem. We expect everyone to ask and answer questions and resolve problems real-time.

For some of our vendors, it's a novel idea. Just recently, I noticed a newly hired consultant use the word "ad hoc" all the time.

AD HOC DUDE: Should I call you next Wednesday, Tim?

TIM: Call me when you have something to show me.

AD HOC DUDE: Okay, I will call you ad hoc.
When can we meet so I can ask questions?
TIM: Post your questions as soon as you think
of them. Don't wait. Somebody will answer
immediately.
AD HOC DUDE: Okay, I will post questions
ad hoc.

Instead of interviewing our people periodically, we use Communifire to stay in touch around the clock. It also serves to let everyone know what everyone else is up to. People can't give you input unless they know what's going on. And the higher up you are, the more input it takes to make a big decision and not regret it later.

Sometimes feedback goes unused. Everyone understands that. It doesn't stop people from weighing in on problems and attempting solutions. Plus, you never know when the same issue will crop up again. We are creating a promotional video now using scripts we wrote two years ago. We had a lot of ideas we didn't use at the time. We are using them now.

Once everyone gets used to it, transparency in the workplace cuts down the need to pry sentiment out of people. The next chapter, *Default to Open*, will show you what that looks like at different companies. In general, open companies take the risk of sharing too much over the risk of missing out on an opportunity to connect, collaborate, and learn. That said, of course, transparency is not all or nothing. You can start small, like this company, for example:

Recreational Equipment, Inc. (REI) was no. 69 on *Fortune's* "100 Best Companies to Work For" in 2014. In 2012, REI launched *Company Campfire*, a social business site, to get employee input and exchange ideas. It started out featuring blog posts by REI executives, employee awards, products and research. Although employees weren't originally invited to blog, they could comment, ask questions, and debate issues.

Google's Laszlo Bock has more advice for beginners:

> *... for any organization, there are four steps you can take to start your own exploration and move from hunches to science: (1) Ask yourself what your most pressing people issues are. Retention? Innovation? Efficiency? Or better yet, ask your people what those issues are. (2) Survey your people about how they think they are doing on those most pressing issues, and what they would do to improve. (3) Tell your people what you learned. If it's about the company, they'll have ideas to improve it. If it's about themselves—like our gDNA work—they'll be grateful. (4) Run experiments based on what your people tell you. Take two groups with the same problem, and try to fix it for just one. Most companies roll out change after change, and never really know why something worked, or if it did at all. By comparing between the groups, you'll be able to learn what works and what doesn't.*[44]

To be a strong leader, you need to know what people think. Ask your people to speak up and listen carefully to what they have to say, but don't expect them to hand you a solution. Steve Jobs said about product design, *"A lot of times, people don't know what they want until you show it to them."* The same is true of inspiring people. Zappos' employees probably didn't ask the management for Bald and Blue days. Nor did Facebook employees ask for a printing press. Those ideas may have come from outside the companies. They've stuck, however, because the leaders stayed in touch, listened, and knew their people well.

CHAPTER 20
DEFAULT TO OPEN

❝ No gossiping. No intrigue. No pussy-footing around problems, and no telling people what you think they want to hear whilst privately disagreeing. We will be transparent in our dealings. **❞**

— THE BOOK OF REDGATE, What we believe in #8/13: No politics

❝ We share everything, and trust Googlers to keep the information confidential. **❞**

— LASZLO BOCK, SVP of People Operations, Google

Meeting behind closed doors and rationing out details on a "need to know" basis may sound reasonable and prudent until you run into problems.

What kinds of problems?

Let's see what we've got in our Biggest Challenge at Work bag. Aha! Here it is:

Job Title	Biggest Challenge at Work
Duty Manager, Operations Center	*"Building trust"*
Senior Human Resources Consultant	*"Communicating effectively so employees trust you"*
Senior Research Officer	*"Distrust of management"*
Equal Employment Director	*"Rebuilding trust between employees and managers"*
Employment Specialist	*"TRUST"*

You want trust? Try being straight with people.

Remember back in Chapter 2, *Hire Traits and Behaviors*, we talked about new hires. When they first set foot at your company, most people have an open mind and a hope to do well. In time and under favorable conditions, these attitudes should blossom into mutual understanding and ripen into trust. Apparently, that's not what is happening at the companies we just heard from. Why not?

Somewhere, somehow, people got the impression that management was out to screw them. This has happened at every company I've worked for and many others I've heard about from my dad, my brother, my friends and coworkers. They all thought the company cared about nothing but profits, and the management's job was to work people to the bone and pay them as little as possible. This was not just a private opinion. It was common lore. "Asshole," "dickhead," "fuckface," "fuckers" and "cocksuckers" are a few of the loving nicknames these people reserved for their higher-ups. Generations of disgruntled employees passed them down, old-timer to new hire.

So, how do you transform culture and lead by example when you go by "that asshole" (boss) or "cocksuckers" (management collectively)?

It's useless to protest your innocence. People's perceptions are their reality. It's better to ask yourself: where exactly did the wires get crossed? And if you look closely, you'll see a series of decisions the leaders made without consulting the people whose livelihood was at stake.

If you are serious about building trust, try eliminating the causes of mistrust. What employee hopes has the company dashed in the past? Can you take responsibility—or, at least, acknowledge the damage? What's eating at your people these days? Can you help them? What fears do they have for the future? Can you allay them now? Make this a true dialogue and watch out for the one-sided tactics that cost you their trust in the first place.

For example, it might be tempting to issue a memo to the effect that from now on the company will do good by the employees and will abstain from doing evil. You could take your time wordsmithing your message and running it by legal. Will it inspire trust? Not likely. If you are not willing to take even a little risk to show trust in your people, don't expect any on their part.

However, a spontaneous and unscripted dialogue, in whatever form your company can manage it, can work a small miracle. In the previous chapter we talked a lot about giving employees a voice to speak their minds. What about the company's voice? Does management ever speak its mind in front of the people? Or does "the voice" come down filtered through layers of censorship and bureaucracy?

If you are in the latter camp, check out this complaint from a recent free-downloader. Does it sound familiar?

Job Title	Biggest Challenge at Work	What brings you to our website?
VP of HR	*"To communicate the HR Policies in un-corrupted form so that the intent of the policies is well understood by all"*	*"Confusion and misunderstanding being created due to ambiguity on certain issues"*

Listen to this VP of HR and learn to speak "in un-corrupted form." Be candid and direct with your people. The upside is well worth it. The 2013 TINYpulse *Employee Engagement Survey* says that 94 percent of happy workplaces practice transparent management. The survey firm, TINYhr, has collected anonymous responses from more than 150 global employers. Here's what they found:

Employee Happiness follows this metric:	% of the time
Transparency of Management	93.7%
Rating of Co-workers Team Members	92.8%
Relationships with Co-Workers	91.6%
Effectiveness of Responding to Feedback	91.6%
Rating of Direct Supervisor	74.3%
Rating of Company Culture	35.1%

Source: TINYpulse.com Engagement Survey. © 2013

Not only was management transparency highly predictive of how people felt about their jobs, it was the chief contributing factor! Coworkers, supervisors, and influence over the company's affairs all came in as runners up.

What's more, transparency seems to impact overall performance. In his book, *Transparency: Creating a Culture of Candor*, Warren Bennis cites a 2005 study of the twenty-seven "most transparent" companies in the U.S. The study group beat the S&P 500 by 11.3 percent.

Wait a minute! How do you run a company without keeping your cards close to your vest?

Google claims to know how:

> *We strive to maintain the open culture often associated with startups, in which everyone is a hands-on contributor and feels comfortable sharing ideas and opinions. In our weekly all-hands ("TGIF")*

meetings—not to mention over email or in the cafe—Googlers ask questions directly to Larry, Sergey and other execs about any number of company issues. Our offices and cafes are designed to encourage interactions between Googlers within and across teams, and to spark conversation about work as well as play.[45]

Google seems to be saying that it's all just a matter of being a startup at heart. It may be true in their case. But don't be fooled into thinking that big corporations are the only ones lacking transparency. They are not. In a now notorious incident, Nolan Bushnell, the founder of Atari, offered young Steve Jobs $5,000 to design a circuit board. Jobs asked Steve Wozniak, a close friend and future co-founder of Apple, for help. He promised to split the bonus 50–50, except he told Woz that the bonus was $700. When Woz delivered the goods, he got paid $350, and Jobs kept $4,650. Back then Apple was not even a startup. It was truly nothing more than a twinkle in Jobs' eye. Steve Jobs never meant for his Apple to be an open and transparent company, and it would never become that way, no matter how big or small it got.

Lack of transparency is not a corporate problem. It's a human problem.

Yes, it's easier to keep people in the loop when there is just a handful of them around—but only if you choose to do so in the first place. Before you worry about mixing employees and management together, as Google does, management has to be willing to show its hand and account for its choices. The temptation to hide your tracks can overwhelm the best of us. It's your survival instincts against your higher self. Gray wolf vs. white wolf. And it has nothing to do with headcount.

My first brush with startup culture was everything but open and comfortable. Axero would have been a different company today, had I not been screwed by my two previous startups.

When I finished my project for the Pennsylvania State Treasury, my manager told me it was going to save the state millions of dollars. He offered to renew my contract, but I turned him down. I figured I'd rather try to make millions for myself. I sold what little I had, dumped my basketball trophies at my parents' house, and drove out to California to join a startup.

My new company was in the hot online auction market. It was a kind of eBay for Dummies. The founder, let's call him "Honest Abe," told me they had physical sites where customers could bring in an item, and the company would list it for them and take a cut when it sold. He told me they already had customers and investors. My job was to build the website, so we could ramp up the business and take the company public. As a partial owner, I'd get a big piece of the action. The future looked bright. I couldn't wait to get started!

When I got there, I found a single drop box store, like Mailboxes, etc., but seedy and dirt-cheap. People came in to ship huge boxes of marijuana. Before I did any programming, I sanded and painted the walls, put in carpeting, and scrubbed the place floor to ceiling. When I started my actual job, I learned that Honest Abe had no cash to pay me. I stuck it out, living on his couch for the next six months.

We were working on computers in the back of the store. Customers always wanted to know what we were doing. Some got psyched and joined the company. There was this buzz in the air—pun intended! More developers came on board. Business picked up. Next I knew, I was writing business plans and pitching to angels and VCs.

I learned early on to watch my back around Honest Abe. But it got worse as we moved closer to Round A. He kept giving us papers to sign that would supersede the papers we had signed earlier. One day I found him rummaging through my files. It became clear that he was trying to cheat us out of our shares. I couldn't sleep. I lost weight. My hair was falling out. To ease the pressure, I started smoking pot, first on the weekends, then long weekends, then for weeks on end. It was hard to give up on the company after all the work and faith I had put into it. But in the end, I had to quit to keep my sanity.

One morning, I pulled up to the store and started packing. Honest Abe's partner, "Modest Gabe," saw me and said, "Wait. Not now." Gabe was one of those entrepreneurial types who talked a blue streak, flashed a little cash, and left it to other people to make good on his promises. He had put $5K into the company and bought himself unlimited access to all the money and talent passing through the doors. "Wait," said Modest Gabe, "I know a guy who might be willing to invest $100K. Let me get him on board, and you and I can strike out on our own. We can do this ourselves."

I was broke and desperate, and I took him at his word. The money actually came through and lasted three years. I occasionally got paid $2,000 a month to build three websites. One was a photo-sharing site, one of the first to hit the Internet. One listed businesses for sale. Another, similar site, was for franchises only. We had no idea which site would make money or how long it would take. Eventually one of them did. Then someone introduced me to VCs. Once again, we were closing in on the Big Time. And, once again, my partner got a little weird.

The seed money ran out. We had a $3M deal in the works, but we needed emergency cash to make it through the next few months. I flew home on a fundraising mission and came back with $50K of my friends' and family's money. Gabe took the money and flew off to India. His official purpose was to buy a software development outfit to get ready for our big round of financing. Three weeks into his trip, I found out that Modest Gabe flew first class and took his whole family on a vacation. The money was gone. Gabe promised Vivek, the guy who had agreed to sell us his company, that he would replace me and take over my shares.

Have you seen one of those movies where the wife and the mistress gang up to kill the husband? Vivek and I compared notes and decided to help each other out of the mess we were in. We hired some legal eagles to go after Modest Gabe. Then we joined up to create a new company, which became Axero. For the next ten years, Vivek and I would bootstrap our own business. No venture capital. No debt. No bullshit.

Right from the start, Vivek and I knew that our company had no chance, unless we could trust each other blindly. I live in San Diego, California. He is halfway around the world, in New Delhi, India. We agreed to be completely open with each other. The same went for everyone who joined the company later on.

Our salespeople have access to all the deals and numbers Axero makes. They can see how much money we are taking in. They can also see where we spend it. The developers can see each other's projects. And anyone can talk to Vivek and me directly.

We have layers of management, like most companies, but we are not hierarchical in the way we communicate.

Needless to say, we were not the only ones shifting from gatekeeping to open collaboration. This shift has been happening for decades in the industry and society. It has now reached the tipping point—which is why Axero is profitable. It's not just the infrastructure that's changing. It's a new way of thinking, which is creating a new way of managing people which, in turn, is calling for new office software and floor plans.

If you want a more transparent workplace, try these two ideas: (1) *Think social*; and (2) *Default to open*.

They can serve as your guiding principles, as you decide what specific measures are right for your company.

THINK SOCIAL

Once upon a time, companies decided in advance what employees needed to know in order to do their jobs. Higher-ups controlled the collective knowledge created by the company and passed it down the food chain through a predetermined set of rules and channels. That was until they realized that existing protocols got in the way of creativity and productivity in the workplace.

Enter social business, and the employee gets to decide what he needs to know, what to share with other employees, and how to learn from them. Social behavior is inherently more engaged, because the employee pulls for information and feedback that would traditionally be pushed his way—or not. It relieves the manager of some of his gatekeeping duties, but it doesn't need to create anarchy and chaos. Managers still manage. And leaders still lead. The idea is to give individuals, managers and execs included, the best opportunity to fulfill on their goals.

DEFAULT TO OPEN

Giving employees direct access to information begs the question: how much? This is obviously something every business needs to decide for itself. However, companies like Google and Red Hat (no. 23 on Glassdoor's "Employees' Choice 50 Best Places to Work" in 2014) ask the question differently.

Instead of deciding what to show and tell people, these companies decide what they want to hide. The rule is that *everyone in the company deserves equal access to information.* In practice, this might mean videotaping CEO staff meetings for the entire company. Or answering tough questions from the audience during a CEO address. Or posting product roadmaps, launch plans, team goals and status reports on the intranet. Or just making it easy for people to get face time and one-on-ones with top management. If you want to make an exception, you'll need a reason why.

Want to see a default-to-open floor plan? Hubspot's boardroom has no doors. Anyone can eavesdrop on clients and execs. Drag in a beanbag chair, get a free beer from the lunchroom, and enjoy! Wait a minute, maybe the boardroom is just for show and the execs meet privately in each other's corner offices? Nope. No offices. Hubspot leaders don't even have assigned desks. They work from wherever they can find an empty spot, and often roam from desk to desk.

The more engaged people are, the more they want to know how the company makes decisions and how they can contribute. One hairy issue is pay and benefits. Companies are notoriously secretive about pay. They think it protects them from jealousy and gossip. In reality, it feeds jealousy and breeds gossip. People always find out, and the only secret is how much they are pissed at management for trying to keep them in the dark.

Luckily, this attitude is starting to shift as well. Whole Foods Market (no. 44 on *Fortune's* "100 Best Companies to Work For" in 2014) lets every one of its 72,000 employees see everyone else's salary. Hiring is another area the company chose to demystify. After a 90-day trial, the entire team votes the new hire in or out. Not only do Whole Foods employees pick new team members, they have a say in their own careers. Every year the company posts thousands of jobs for all to explore. Transparency in pay and promotions helps keep employees happy and promote from within. The company says that 90 percent of the managers, including some of the top execs, got their start somewhere in the store.

One nice perk to being open with people is that you don't need to tell them how to treat customers. People get trained just by being treated right as employees. Our salespeople don't make false promises. When they screw up, they don't pretend it's the customer's fault. If they take a couple of days to respond to an inquiry, they'll say, "Sorry, we forgot about you; your email got buried. Here's the answer to your question." It works!

Building trust in the workplace is not just a noble cause. All the people-management roads lead to trust. What do you do when it's missing? You have to give it to get it. At the very minimum, make it as clear as possible to people how you calculate their pay, how you promote, and how performance makes a difference in their paychecks and careers.

Transparency is the best and most effective way of showing trust. It's not intuitive to most companies, but it's a habit worth taking on. In the words of the American novelist E. W. Howe, *"The man who can keep a secret may be wise, but he is not half as wise as the man with no secrets to keep."*

CHAPTER 21
GO ON A MISSION

"A man always has two reasons for doing anything: a good reason and the real reason."

— J.P. MORGAN

"Go to the people. Live with them. Learn from them. Love them. Start with what they know. Build with what they have. But with the best leaders, when the work is done, the task is accomplished, the people will say, 'We have done this ourselves.'"

— LAO TZU

In 1997, cartoonist Scott Adams and reporter Tia O'Brien played a prank on a group of executives at Logitech International. With the help of Logitech's co-founder Pierluigi Zappacosta, Adams passed himself off as a consultant, hired to fine-tune the mission statement for the company's New Ventures Group. Adams tells the story in his book *The Joy of Work*:

> *I had two specific goals for the meeting: 1) Lead the executives into creating the longest, most useless, buzzword-heavy mission statement on earth. 2) Get volunteers to agree to put the mission statement to music ...*

Adams starts the meeting off by establishing his credentials: his fictitious Harvard MBA and his fictitious expertise with household name brands. He slips in a little sarcasm, which goes off completely unnoticed:

> *I explained that while working at P&G I had discovered through research that people often tasted the detergents and cleansers before using them. My job was to improve the taste of all soap products. There were murmurs of approval at this "out of box" thinking.*

Assured of the group's high tolerance towards corporate nonsense, Adams proceeds with his plan. Within an hour, he gets the executives to produce the following:

> **Mission Statement:** *The New Ventures Mission is to scout profitable growth opportunities in relationships, both internally and externally, in emerging, mission-inclusive markets, and explore new paradigms and then filter and communicate and evangelize the findings.*

Next, he sets the stage for the grand finale: getting the execs to sing.

> *I explained that although this might seem silly on the surface, there is a wealth of evidence that people can remember words more easily if they are put to music. Two executives confessed to having musical*

talents, and—since they were team players—they
agreed to take on the task of the musical mission
statement. Mercifully, I ripped off the wig and
mustache and revealed my true identity ...

Of course, there was nothing wrong with the Logitech execs. It could have been any company—well, just about. Nor is there anything wrong with having a mission statement. If you are on a mission that gives meaning and purpose to your day, why not declare it to the world?

And that's a big "if."

The problem is that we are so used to stating all kinds of fake missions and visions, that we can't even tell the real thing from a sarcastic prank. I am the first one to be guilty of that. And I have a story to prove it.

In 2008, roughly ten years after Adams' experiment at Logitech, Vivek and I hired a consultant to write our business plan. We had just been washed up high and dry on the great wild shores of Startupland. Our ongoing mission was to refill our bank account before the next payroll. Anyone who dangled "investors" in front of our noses got our attention.

Our consultant recommended we put a mission statement into the business plan. Like the Logitech execs, we were eager to say whatever he thought would impress the bigwigs. Unlike Adams, our consultant did not rip off his wig and reveal his true nature. So, we paid his bill, and the mission statement went into our business plans and on our website, where it sat for six years without drawing any attention whatsoever.

Vivek and I never got our big cash infusion, but work came in here and there. We took all kinds of projects just to make ends meet—and tinkered with our software in our spare time. Finally, the day came when we felt free to choose the kind of work we did. We chose to focus on Communifire and share it with as many people as we could. Once we took a stand on the direction of our business, our reasons became clear, too. All this time we spent in team meetings and project updates, we were learning how our clients and employees liked to work. How we liked to work. We wanted to use that knowledge. We wanted to come to people and say, "Here. Try this. We think you'll like it."

In 2014, we finally got around to updating our website. After the Home Page, the second most viewed page was About Us. And there it was, our gift to the world and the reason to drop whatever you were doing and come join our team:

> *To improve collaboration for enterprises and communities through the real-world application of social networking tools and approaches.*

What?

My eyes couldn't focus on the page, and I couldn't make any sense of it, no matter how many times I read it. It was nothing like us, and it said nothing about us. It was about somebody hiding behind plausible gibberish, hoping to blend in with every other company out there.

I showed the page to Raja, a friend of mine who happened to be a world-class pro in all things branding.

> TIM: How do we even talk about ourselves
> without sounding like a bunch of wannabes?

My parents always told me: don't talk about
yourself, be modest.
RAJA: Just sit down and write something, Tim.
Throw the old page away and start from scratch.
Write full sentences and start every sentence with
"We."

So that's what I did, and in about fifteen minutes I had
the following:

WE ARE AXERO:

1. We are on a mission to enable people to lead their
   own social initiatives.

2. We are extremely passionate—we love what we do.

3. We are based in sunny San Diego, but we work
   from all over the globe.

4. We believe that social software isn't about technology—it's about people.

5. We value transparency, respect, and sincerity in
   everything we do.

6. We consider pleasing customers the most important
   part of our job.

7. We listen to you, our customers, who drive our
   product innovation.

8. We're a small company that works very hard to
   keep your trust.

9. We are profitable and debt free.

10. We owe neither money nor allegiance to anyone else.

11. We owe everything to our customers.

We added a picture of the Coronado Bridge and turned it live. Our people were psyched. Customers called us to say that the new page made sense. They said that we wore our hearts on our sleeves, and now so did the website. We were surprised, but we liked it. So, we went ahead and put in a heart symbol where it said "love."

It goes to show that being yourself counts, even when you don't think you have much to brag about. It took me ten years—all of Axero's history and beyond—to get to what I wrote. And, even though it's hardly original and still pretty cheesy, somehow our customers and employees knew that it was for real.

If a simple brain dump can serve as a bonding tool between you and your people, imagine what a truly insightful self-portrait can do. And, if you have thousands of brilliant employees at your disposal, then shame on you if you can't get them to produce a timeless masterpiece. Like this one, for example:

> *Ten things we know to be true: We first wrote these "10 things" when Google was just a few years old. From time to time we revisit this list to see if it still holds true. We hope it does—and you can hold us to that.*
>
> *1.   Focus on the user and all else will follow ...*
>
> *2.   It's best to do one thing really, really well ...*
>
> *3.   Fast is better than slow ...*
>
> *4.   Democracy on the web works ...*

5. *You don't need to be at your desk to need an answer ...*

6. *You can make money without doing evil ...*

7. *There's always more information out there ...*

8. *The need for information crosses all borders ...*

9. *You can be serious without a suit ...*

10. *Great just isn't good enough ...*[46]

By the way, neither Google's piece nor ours is a mission statement. But if you are going to end up with something unique and revealing, it's good to start with what you know. From there, you can decide how to organize your thoughts, and what to call them. You may not even end up with a mission statement at all. What's important is that the words you choose pull your company together for a purpose.

Which brings me back to my original point: being on a mission and having a mission statement are two different things.

Your mission is something you feel strongly about, even if you don't say it out loud. It's personal. And it shows in the choices you make day in and day out. Your mission can be a reason to come to work, put up with bullshit—or not— think on your feet, solve problems, partner with people, and be creative. Consistently acting on your beliefs puts you on a mission. The following is just one example of what I think being on a mission looks like.

In 1970, rock climber Yvon Chouinard brought regulation team rugby shirts from his trip to Scotland. The shirts were a big hit with his climbing buddies in California, and many more people asked for them. This prompted Chouinard, who was already manufacturing climbing gear, to start a second company, dedicated to clothing. Besides the shirts, Patagonia, Inc. sold polyurethane windbreakers, bivouac sacks from Scotland, boiled-wool mittens from Austria, and hand-knit reversible hats from Boulder. The company threw "blasphemously" bright colors into the gray and khaki world of serious outdoor clothing, and caused a minor fashion revolution.

Chouinard used Patagonia's money and fame to protect the things he loved and wanted other people to explore: nature and wildlife. He started close to home, by saving Los Angeles' Ventura River and its steelhead salmon population from imminent death by urban expansion. In 1986, Patagonia committed 10 percent of profits to environmental causes, and soon upped the bid to 1 percent of sales, if greater. They have followed through every year since. In the early 1990s, the company learned through independent research that cotton, used in most of its clothing, was responsible for 25 percent of all toxic pesticides on the planet. The damage from conventionally grown cotton was (and is) shocking. Between 1994 and 1996, Patagonia switched to all-organic cotton.

When daily minutiae drowns out your principles, a few well-chosen words can put you back on track. And this is where a mission statement comes in. Here's Patagonia's:

> *Build the best product, cause no unnecessary harm,*
> *use business to inspire and implement solutions to*
> *the environmental crisis.*[47]

So, how do you explain everything you do and everything you believe in just a couple of sound bites? Well, you don't.

The companies we've looked at go into a lot more detail than the formulaic history-mission-vision-values. To continue with Patagonia's example, they spell out their *Reason for Being*:

> *Patagonia grew out of a small company that made tools for climbers. Alpinism remains at the heart of a worldwide business that still makes clothes for climbing—as well as for skiing, snowboarding, surfing, fly fishing, paddling and trail running. These are all silent sports. None requires a motor; none delivers the cheers of a crowd. In each sport, reward comes in the form of hard-won grace and moments of connection between us and nature. Our values reflect those of a business started by a band of climbers and surfers, and the minimalist style they promoted. The approach we take towards product design demonstrates a bias for simplicity and utility. For us at Patagonia, a love of wild and beautiful places demands participation in the fight to save them, and to help reverse the steep decline in the overall environmental health of our planet. We donate our time, services and at least 1% of our sales to hundreds of grassroots environmental groups all over the world who work to help reverse the tide. We know that our business activity—from lighting stores to dyeing shirts—creates pollution as a by-product. So we work steadily to reduce those harms. We use recycled polyester in many of our clothes and only organic, rather than pesticide-intensive, cotton.*

> *Staying true to our core values during thirty-plus*
> *years in business has helped us create a company*
> *we're proud to run and work for. And our focus*
> *on making the best products possible has brought*
> *us success in the marketplace.*[48]

When they remind you of what you already believe, words can ground and inspire. When they remind you of a third-rate billboard, they do the opposite. Do you think Patagonia would have achieved the same effect with *"We are helping people improve lives one <insert your company's product here> at a time"*?

Supposing your company is on a mission, go ahead and put it into words, pictures or artifacts, like our friends at Facebook, Zappos, Redgate, and other companies have done. Look deep inside your own soul or use the crowdsourcing tactics we've talked about in Chapter 19 to find the right words.

But what if your company isn't on a mission, not the kind you want to splash all over your collateral, anyway? Well then, don't repeat my mistake and pay an outsider to manufacture one for you. Find a better use for your money. Pierluigi Zappacosta from Logitech had the right idea: bring in a comedian and have a good laugh at everyone else's expense!

I, for one, always stumble when people ask me what I do for a living, let alone what my mission is. "What do you do, Tim?" "Ummmmm ... yeah. I own a software company ... I do a lot of marketing and write some code ..." At this point my girlfriend, Kimberly, usually jumps in, if she is in the room. "Tim, you do way more than that!" Whatever I do doesn't feel like a job. It's a happy feeling. And it's how I want everyone to feel, at least when they are working for me or using my software.

Even though I can't tell you what our mission statement is, most of the time I can tell what it isn't. Ever since we've published our new About Us page, I've been getting calls from VCs. Apparently, they like the smell of "profitable and debt-free," and want to sniff out our financials. "Are you making $5 million yet? We can take it from there, explode the company and take it public." Thanks, but it's not a priority right now.

That's another thing to keep in mind. Rubber-stamp mission statements are *inclusive*. They try to appeal to everyone. By contrast, the real mission, the one you've been on all along, has nothing to do with appeasing your critics. It's about reaching those already on the same wavelength with you. They will get it loud and clear.

A true mission is bound to leave somebody out. Find out what's important to people who are already in your corner. Don't chase hypothetical fans and don't try to cement your mission for all possible versions of the future. Your mission is a moving target. It will change as you grow and learn.

Ours was about surviving. Then it was about social networking. Then social business. Then collaboration, intranets, and online workspaces. Now it's about bringing people together to work smarter—and building a workplace they can claim as their own.

Discover your mission, don't fake it. Even if there are a million companies doing the same thing you do, find what's in it for you and your people. Here's Google again:

> *Other companies make similar products, and yet our employees tell us that they are drawn to Google because being here means something more than "just"*

searching the internet or linking friends. (Laszlo
Bock, svp of People Operations, Google, Passion
not Perks, thinkwithgoogle.com, September 2011)

Google started by searching out what excited employees
about their work. *"If we were motivated by money,"* says CEO
Larry Page, *"we would have sold the company a long time ago and
ended up on a beach."* They decided their mission was to *"organize
the world's information and to make it universally accessible and
useful."* Is it really? Well, judge for yourself.

On January 25 of 2011, when the news of the Egyptian
revolution broke out, a few Google employees decided to do
something to help people in Egypt stay connected during those
trying times. Over the weekend, a small team of engineers
from Google and Twitter came up with a service enabling
anyone to tweet by leaving a voicemail. On Monday, January
31, *Speak2Tweet* went live with three international phone numbers that would instantly tweet the message using the hashtag
#egypt, no Internet connection required. People could listen
to the messages by dialing the same phone numbers or going
to twitter.com/speak2tweet. On February 1, Google updated
Speak2Tweet with country-specific hashtags, depending on the
origin of the call.

In short, companies succeed by putting themselves on
a mission. A mission neither begins nor ends with a mission
statement. Words themselves are not as important as where they
come from. Did you crowdsource your mission statement—or
did you let a top executive hammer it out? Did you take a fresh
look at your company, your business, and your market—or did
you rehash old rhetoric? Does your mission statement reflect

how your people feel about their jobs—or does it merely satisfy marketing and HR?

Likewise, spreading the word is less important than putting it into everyday practice.

Says Laszlo Bock, *"The translation of our mission into something real and tangible has a huge effect on who decides to join Google, how much engagement and creativity they bring to this place, and even on how they feel and behave after leaving."*

CHAPTER 22
ENGAGE OUTSIDE OF WORK

"A man should keep on being constructive, and do constructive things. He should take part in the things that go on in this wonderful world.**"**

— J. WILLARD MARRIOTT

"I do environmental compliance work, and I have a passion for recycling and reuse. So I wanted to help out with the event. I was on the planning committee, and I was in charge of getting the pizza and the gloves and communicating to my plant. I actually really enjoy it.**"**

— MILA DEMPSEY, Environmental Manager, Cummins Inc.[49]

Being on a mission feels good and works well. The only problem is that you can't fake it. Try it once, and people respond with fakery of their own. Fake nods, fake enthusiasm, fake team-playing. How did they know to put on their nine-to-five faces and go into hiding? What tipped them off?

Here's an easy test. Are you still on a mission when you leave the office? Does your mission count where it doesn't directly boost your bottom line? Mission implies commitment. Commitment takes character. And character doesn't take time off or require compensation. That's how they know.

If you really care and are not just wearing one of your annoying corporate "hats," you will support your cause for its own sake on your own time. When you do that, it shows character. When others follow, it builds character for the entire company.

It may seem counterintuitive to take people volunteering on the weekends, when they are already sick of putting in regular hours for good pay. But there is a reason why it works and why companies do it. Some even pay their employees to volunteer.

Engine maker Cummins Inc. (no. 20 on *Forbes'* "25 Best Places to Work" in 2014) involves more than half of its 47,900 employees in local community projects. In 2013, Cummins donated 308,783 hours, about ten hours per participating employee. The company treats volunteering as a business function, headed by a VP of Corporate Responsibility.

And the payoff?

Cummins believes that volunteering together strengthens relationships between managers and workers and leads to higher engagement and productivity at work.

Management consultants at Boston Consulting Group (no. 3 on *Fortune's* "100 Best Companies to Work For" in 2014) frequently donate their time to the U.N. World Food Program, Save the Children and other philanthropies. In the wake of the 2010 earthquake in Haiti, BCG took consultants off client projects so they could volunteer in disaster areas.

SAP, one of the world's largest business software companies (no. 42 on Glassdoor's "Employees' Choice 50 Best Places to Work" in 2013), employs 66,000 people on six continents. In 2012, SAP launched its Social Sabbatical to help entrepreneurs and small businesses in disadvantaged communities. When employees sign up for the program, they get a fully paid 4-week leave of absence to serve at startup incubators and non-profits around the world. Internal surveys say that, when they come back from Social Sabbaticals, employees are *"more motivated to perform"* and *"proud to work for SAP."*

People may be judging your company by its good works even before they come on board. Especially the younger crowd. A study by AMP Agency found that 61 percent of the Millennials support social causes. And more than half would not take a job unless the employer shared their beliefs.

They may all have a point. The story I'm about to tell you takes us back to the fall of 2007. Even after so many years, it still sends chills down my spine as I write it down.

At the end of October, I went to Pennsylvania, as I do every fall, to visit family and watch the leaves change color. I was flying back to San Diego when the plane got close to the ground and everyone's eyes turned to the windows. It was dark. But instead of the usual pattern of electric lights, we saw flames. Lots of them, burning in long stretches in every direction. We were flying into the heart of the southern California wildfires of 2007. Everyone on the plane started talking. First to the person sitting next to them. Then to the neighbors across the aisle. Pretty soon everyone was talking to everyone.

It's easy to meet people on the plane. You talk. You make a connection … And you never see each other again. Edward Norton's character in *Fight Club* called them "single-serving friends." That evening I met people who knew that their businesses and homes had already burned down. When I stepped off the plane, I was leaving behind dozens of single-serving friends. In need. And thousands more like them as far as the eye could see. I couldn't just leave it at that.

I went home and turned on the TV. The fires were getting closer by the minute, and the newscasters couldn't get the updates out fast enough. At the time, I was working on my second start-up, building all kinds of websites. Suddenly, it dawned on me that I might know how to help.

I registered the domain, californiawildfires.org. The website is now defunct, but you can still find links to it on the Internet. Next, I threw up a Wordpress blog and started posting bits and pieces of information as it was coming in from local TV, radio, and news websites. Everyone in the company pitched in. We posted all the breaking news. Every piece of advice. How to help, and where to find help. Links. Addresses. Phone numbers. Hero stories.

The site instantly shot to the no. 1 position in Google for the keyword "California wildfires." Suddenly, our phone started ringing. Someone found our company name on the copyright section of the blog, followed the links to our company site and called us for help. After that, we added our phone number to the new website. In the next few days, I hardly slept. We were getting calls at 4:00 a.m.!

Since people were calling, I told the local authorities about the website. They fed us information to post and we became *the* go-to resource for the fires. Multiple TV stations broadcast our web address. Everyone in the company did everything possible to keep the helpline going, without being asked. I was in the middle of the disaster area. Others were out of harm's way in northern California, Canada, and across the Pacific. But the distance made no difference. We put all other projects on hold, and for a few days, until the fires subsided, we were a whole different kind of company. Beyond connected. Beyond productive. Beyond engaged.

So what? You are probably wondering what happened after the fires. Did our selfless endeavor attract major investors or at least score some new business? Nope. Nothing at all, businesswise. What's more, without other humanitarian projects to follow, the selflessness quickly disappeared. And, before the inch-thick layer of ash in my driveway had melted away, it was all backstabbing as usual.

You already know the sad end of my second startup. Californiawildfires.org was, hands-down, the best thing we ever did as a company. It may even be the best thing I've ever done in my life. And that may explain the rise of corporate volunteering better than any chart-backed HR report. Do you want your people to feel good about themselves? In that case, nothing will yield more collective self-worth than selflessly helping others. The more often you do it, the better the odds it will stick and become the rule for everything your people do at work.

FIND YOUR NICHE AS A VOLUNTEER

Taking up a cause may come naturally, like environmental activism to Patagonia. The company pays employees to work full-time on local environmental projects. But it can also be a struggle. I have to tell you my own cautionary tale here.

When I help people, it's usually friends building websites— because they ask me. I say yes, and then I kick myself for over-committing. Nevertheless, one time I decided to expand my reach and benefit a larger portion of humanity.

Kimberly and I got together with another couple and made sandwiches to feed the homeless. We bought one hundred brown paper bags and filled them with sandwiches, chips, and oranges.

We took the bags to downtown San Diego and started looking for hungry people we could feed.

It's not hard to find homeless in San Diego, if you know where to look. There were some on the streets and whole communities camping under the bridges. Giving the food away was a different story. It was like starting a business. The first three attempts ended in failure. I think I took more rejection that day than during the rest of my life put together. It went like this:

1ST ATTEMPT

TIM: Hi there! Would you like a sandwich?

HOMELESS PERSON #1: What kind of a sandwich is this?

TIM: Bologna and cheese.

HOMELESS PERSON #1: No, I don't like it.

2ND ATTEMPT

TIM: Hello! Would you like a sandwich and an orange?

HOMELESS PERSON #2: What kind of sandwich?

TIM: Bologna and cheese.

HOMELESS PERSON #2: No, thanks. I just had one. They are giving them out over there.

3RD ATTEMPT

TIM: How about you, would you like a bologna and cheese sandwich?

HOMELESS PERSON #3: They are grilling hamburgers around the corner. I think I'll have a hamburger.

What was I thinking? People of San Diego obviously knew their food and gave our bologna and cheese nothing but well-deserved contempt. We kept scouring the city for classless bums who would be willing to take a bite of our sandwiches. Some people we met already had brown paper bags. Some refused to take "our leftovers." I gave a few sandwiches to guys under the bridge wearing designer clothes and carrying new laptops and iPads. Eventually we gave them all away, except the one or two I ate myself. And that was the last time I helped the homeless. Next time, I'll try the elderly or the kids.

Would your people like to volunteer—but you don't know where to start? I think starting locally is a good idea. But making an asshole out of yourself isn't. Please avoid my mistake and do your research first. Supply and demand still count, even when the price is "free." Ask your people. Chances are, some of them are already doing it on their own. During the warmer months, look into outdoor activities like cleaning up a park or helping a local organic farmer. If you have multiple locations, you can contract with companies like Taproot or Catchafire to place employee teams on projects all over the U.S.

... OR JUST HAVE FUN

Of course, volunteering is not the only way for your employees to get to know and trust one another. Sports and social activities can also do the trick. As early as 1914, IBM CEO Thomas J. Watson created employee sports teams and hosted family outings, complete with a company band.

Some companies worry that too much socializing can lead to employee dating and hookups. Of course it can, and it does. And why not? Would you rather have sexual frustration on top of all the work stress? I am not saying give out condoms in the cafeteria, but give your people some space!

Social is where it is for us at Axero right now. Not surprisingly—because we are all about social, anyway. We've created a social-social space inside of our social intranet platform. It's our Water Cooler. Everyone's invited. Post whatever you want.

Many people post music and recommend movies and books. We have seasonal themes, like gift ideas. And, of course, photos. People sharing little pieces of themselves to overcome weirdness and connect human-to-human. All of this is bond-building and de-stressing, and you want it on your intranet.

A purely social site on the intranet also gives rise to spontaneous giving. We don't have to organize anything. We just give it space and our collective blessing. Bryce likes to donate blood. Not something I'm into, but I am grateful someone else is. He gets a full day off to do it. He also gets to post pictures of himself and his donations. The photos are pretty gross if you ask me, but maybe they motivate other people. So we might have a blood drive going on at the company, and I don't even have to know about it.

Like everything else we've talked about, corporate volunteering only works when people choose it for themselves, not when management forces it down their throats. The same goes for corporate fun. Take initiative. Set an example. But tread lightly where it comes to enrolling your people. Best of all, give them the freedom to join their own causes.

CHAPTER 23
SAY THANK YOU

❝ We often take for granted the very things that most deserve our gratitude. ❞
— CYNTHIA OZICK, American writer

❝ Treat employees like they make a difference—and they will. ❞
— JIM GOODNIGHT, Founder and CEO, SAS

Acknowledgement works. It is the quickest way to restore trust, transform a strained relationship, or energize the whole workplace. The ripple effect of every "thank you" is astronomical. Anything you can do to show sincere gratitude to employees will come back a hundredfold.

But what can you do beyond the simple *give-credit-where-credit-is-due* and *do-as-your-mother-taught-you*?

It turns out that you can do a lot. Companies who beat the market by being nice to employees have added entire dimensions to saying thanks. And even though one company's habits rarely match the needs of another, saying thank you is a special case. You can take any one of these ideas into your company tomorrow, and never worry about employee engagement again. They are that powerful. Here they are.

Gratitude dimension #1: Thank your people for weird stuff when they least expect it

Like making mistakes. Before Sheryl Sandberg became the COO of Facebook, she worked at Google. Her job was important enough that one of her mistakes cost Google several million dollars. When she told Larry Page about it, his reaction surprised her:

> *"I'm so glad you made this mistake," he said. "Because I want to run a company where we are moving too quickly and doing too much, not being too cautious and doing too little. If we don't have any of these mistakes, we're just not taking enough risk."*[50]

Any company looking for fresh ideas to rise above its peers can take a cue from Google. Thank employees for taking a risk, even if they fail, and you may create a fearless office culture, where people are free to think big and challenge one another. When you express gratitude for bold, courageous action, you also encourage people to own and share their mistakes, so that everyone can learn from them.

Gratitude dimension #2: Make it social

"Thank you" does not need to come down the chain of command. It can come from anywhere. Besides, the top brass isn't there day-to-day to see all the grunt work. Even the front-line managers don't see and appreciate all the effort.

There is no question that managers need to know and acknowledge their people. However, it's even more important that coworkers acknowledge each other. The 2013 TINYpulse

Employee Engagement Survey reports that coworkers contribute more to employee happiness than do the bosses. The study found a 92 percent correlation between employee happiness and their rating of coworkers, compared to a 74 percent correlation between employee happiness and their rating of their direct supervisors.

How can you make sure that no good deed goes unnoticed? Put a system in place that encourages employees to thank one another. My girlfriend, Kimberly, works for Scripps, a private healthcare provider. She is a nurse and she loves her job. Whenever she helps out her coworkers, she gets a thank you card from them. It's a form that anyone can fill out, patients, too. After it's been filled out, the card goes to the management, and then back to Kimberly.

A simple thanks is great, but a card is something she can bring home with her and hang on the fridge. Every time she does, we talk about it, and I can see how good it makes her feel. Having these cards on hand, she is more likely to thank someone else, too, because she can see all the difference they make in her life—and ours together.

As you see, *social* doesn't always imply high-tech electronic media. But if your company does use a social business or intranet platform, you know it's great for spreading gratitude. Take Philips, for example. Philips North America has built peer-to-peer recognition into its social intranet. *Connect Us* is available on desktops and as a mobile app and has "Thanks badges" for employees to publicly acknowledge their coworkers.

Gratitude dimension #3: Connect the dots

Kimberly and I both enjoy her thank you cards. But the company's flow of gratitude doesn't stop there. Scripps lets employees collect points for every thank you card they receive and for various other achievements. The points are good for all kinds of products at the company's online store, not just branded company swag. So, she gets to pick her own reward. Her choice? A footbath.

Gratitude dimension #4: Have your own special ways of expressing gratitude

This one takes a little creativity and a lot of knowing your people. Give it some thought. What will make your people feel important, understood, and treasured for their special gifts and contributions?

Camden Trust likes to give hugs. Starbucks launched a special card collection from a mobile app Red Stamp, so that customers can thank their baristas by mail, email or social media. LinkedIn bought 3,458 iPad Minis to thank all of its full-time employees for their hard work.

Nobody likes a thankless job. If management doesn't make people feel appreciated, many employees will correct the oversight by helping themselves to products and supplies or giving themselves a day off. Next thing you know, you have theft and absenteeism on your hands, and saying thank you is the last thing on your mind.

Thank your employees first, before they thank themselves. You don't need a special occasion. Thank them for being employees. For coming in to work and taking care of business. For putting up with you and your ways of running the company. Remember, there is always more than meets the eye. You cannot walk in every employee's shoes, nor can you fight everyone's battles. Thank them for things you don't know about, and you won't be wrong. Encourage everyone at your company to say thank you. Invest in a system that lets employees instantly and publicly settle their debts of gratitude.

If you are looking for happy, hard-working people, never skimp on encouragement.

Thank you for reading this chapter.

CHAPTER 24

GIVE THEM A BREAK

❝ Only two rules really count. Never miss an opportunity to relieve yourself; never miss a chance to sit down and rest your feet. ❞

— EDWARD VIII

❝ BOSTON GLOBE: Do any of you offer unlimited vacation time?
BRUNNER: We used to offer that, and then we hired a CFO. ❞

— LESLIE BRUNNER, SVP of people and process, Athenahealth

Our lives move in cycles. Eat-poop. Buy-sell. Wake up, go to bed. Of all the cycles, the succession of activity and rest may be the most fundamental. In theory, we understand how this works, and why we sometimes need to put down the most urgent task and the most captivating challenge until we are ready to resume. In practice, we often ignore the obvious. We get caught up in the moment. We get into a rut. We get stressed, anxious, excited, fearful, greedy, obsessed—and then we slave-drive people around us. Worst of all, we slave-drive ourselves.

The theory behind taking breaks from work is simple. Work takes effort. Effort wears and tears down the worker. Wear and tear diminish the worker's capacity for physical, mental, and moral effort. If you want full effort, you must stop work until the capacity is fully restored.

You cannot escape the wear-and-tear cycle. Your only choice is the kind of cycle you will have. You could have a healthy cycle where you and your employees come to work fully recharged—or you could have a vicious cycle that drains productivity and good will right out of your company. Like this one, for example:

> ... *The company installed a bathroom tracking system, in which employees swipe their* ID *cards to get into the bathroom, earlier this year. Union members say that last month, managers began routinely disciplining workers who were using the bathroom more than 6 minutes per day ... [The company's] philosophy is that they feel like people are getting an extra break in the bathroom, said union representative Kreitman.*[51]

Of course, the company and its policies are only one part of the equation. The employees and their individual habits are the other part. However, as we've seen throughout this book, a company can do a lot to set the right tone and create new habits in the workplace.

What kinds of habits are we talking about?

Every production cycle needs a built-in rest and recharge period. Think of it as maintenance. Your car has 5-, 10-, 15-, 30-, and 50-thousand mile service plans. Skip one and you risk accidents and expensive repairs. What about your people and all of their moving parts—eyes, hands, feet, hearts and minds? How often do they need preventive maintenance?

Most people plan their time in annual, weekly and daily cycles. There are also projects and tasks. Let's go through all of them one by one.

ANNUAL CYCLE

The annual breaks include holidays, vacations, and other paid time off, like sick and personal days. How you parcel it out says a lot about your company. If you keep close tabs on how your people spend their time off and save longer vacations for managers and long-term employees, then you probably don't think your employees are all that excited about coming to work. And you may be right about that. A place where mature adults can't decide how to best take care of themselves and their business is disempowering and depressing.

A company that blindly trusts all employees to take time off when they need it tells a different story. The assumption here is that everyone does more than his fair share, and the concern is not how to keep people at work, but how to make sure they get enough rest. This may sound utopian, but some companies do make it a reality.

According to the Society for Human Resource Management (SHRM) 2013 survey, *Paid Leave in the Workplace*, 2 percent of employers provide unlimited vacations; 5 percent of employers provide unlimited personal leave; 6 percent of employers provide unlimited paid time off; and 12 percent of employers provide unlimited sick leave.

Who are these companies? Well, Axero for one, but also Netflix, Glassdoor, Richard Branson's Virgin Group, and a

Seattle-based credit card processing company called Gravity Payments.

Strangely enough, companies are not the only ones resisting the change. Employees who are used to cashing in leftover vacations can go nuts when the company goes unlimited. The unlimited vacation policy at the *Los Angeles Times* was so unpopular that the company had to rescind it only a week after it went into effect. As always, it pays to check in with your folks before you impose a major change, even if it is for their own good.

The flip side of taking time off when you need it is not taking it when you don't need it. Companies who let employees choose their own time off also tend to skip set holidays in favor of a completely personalized schedule. Of course, you have to make sure that your schedule works for your manager, your team, and your client. But with the HR out of the picture, you have one less hoop to jump through.

If you don't like the idea of unlimited vacations, find another way to prevent burnout. Here's Athenahealth:

> ... *Last year I rolled out a sabbatical program. So, after eight years at Athenahealth, every person gets a [one-time] six extra weeks of vacation—and you can do whatever you want. But you have to come back and tell people what you did. If you sat on the couch and watched talk shows, that's fine, but you have to tell it to the entire leadership group.*[52]

WEEKLY CYCLE

Weeks are similar to years in that we expect to work on certain days, like Monday through Friday, and take the weekends off.

But who can get everything done during the week? Projects routinely spill into the weekends. It's even worse if you like your job. Weekends could be your only chance to get caught up on the Second Quadrant: important (and fun) but not urgent. So you spend all day Saturday and Sunday playing with the screen layout for a new feature you think will blow the customer's mind. Monday rolls around—you have a beta ready to test, but you are tired and brain-dead. Take Monday off!!!

DAILY CYCLE

The most important thing we do every day to rest and recharge is sleep. Ideally that should be all we need to get ready for work the next day. Unfortunately, many people go to bed too late, show up to work tired and sleep-deprived day after day, and there goes employee morale, happiness, engagement and contribution.

Getting a good night's sleep is one area where corporate policy-making may not make a big difference. But a personal example at the top will and does. This is why Facebook's Sheryl Sandberg, Arianna Huffington, and other star execs like to talk about sleeping their way to the top.

Not only does caring about basic human needs like rest and sleep inspire your own employees, it can attract others to your company. Here's the story of how Facebook stole its VP of global sales, Carolyn Everson, from Microsoft:

> ... *Sandberg called Everson from her car, from her home, and from vacation in Mexico, where Everson could hear her kids frolicking in the background. "One night she left a message saying she was actually going to bed at 9 or 9:30 and that she was*

exhausted," Everson says. "I was, like, at least this woman sleeps."[53]

Aside from sleep, our bodies need breaks for food and to go to the bathroom. Physiologically speaking, eating at your desk is no better than relieving yourself at your desk. For best results, both functions require concentration and a relaxed setting. Labor unions seem to be ahead of the game in vigorously defending their members' rights to eat and eliminate with dignity and in peace.

Let the rest of us not fall too far behind. There are two ways you can instill healthy habits in the workplace: (1) personal example; and (2) convenience.

We will talk more about setting up your office space for healthy breaks in the next chapter, *Let the Walls Help*. For now, let me just say that personal example is important even when people can't see you, as the case of Sheryl Sandberg and Carolyn Everson clearly demonstrates. People can get a whiff of how you take care of yourself over the phone, online, and through the grapevine—and they will expect you to treat them the same.

PROJECT CYCLE

Projects are why we build companies and hire employees. Most of us are better at starting projects than we are at completing them. So, it's easy to "reward" top performers with more and more work, but it's not always a good idea.

Busy doesn't mean productive, and the relationship between the two is not linear. It's more of a bell curve: after a certain point, the more work you pile on, the less you get done, until you reach one of the—

FOUR STAGES OF BEING OVERWORKED

Stage One: Your entire day is filled with one crisis after another.

Stage Two: Your entire day is spent explaining to people that your entire day is filled with one crisis after another.

Stage Three: Your entire day is spent apologizing for the crises you didn't handle because you spent your entire day explaining to other people that your day was filled with crises.

Stage Four: You're so busy that no one even dares call you.[54]

It's just as important to cut the hard-working people, including yourself, some slack, as it is to light a fire under the slackers. And that's the easy lesson. The hard lesson is how do you do that? Here's my story.

We have an excellent employee, Raghav. He is great at what he does, and, being an agreeable guy, he gets peppered with requests all the time. I used to be the worst offender, adding to his already long to-do list almost daily. I could see that he was always busy, but I used to think that, because I was the CEO, my projects were more important than anybody else's. One day it occurred to me that he already had assigned work. Constant side requests put him over capacity with no end in sight. Not good. I was burning out the employee I couldn't afford to lose. Right then and there I decided to stop. I still go to Raghav for help sometimes, but only with small tasks that take under an hour that I absolutely need done right away.

Don't let your people jump from one project to another in crisis mode. Give them downtime between major assignments. Teach them to break up big complicated projects into clear and manageable tasks. Don't pile on work, simply because they are up to the task. And, finally, look for signs of being overwhelmed and learn to set people's minds at ease. More often than work itself, it's the thought of a larger-than-life workload that brings us down.

TASK CYCLE

Even individual tasks move along faster if we understand how to break them up. It's not just about putting down the work. Often, we can get the break we need by changing our environment, our mental focus, or the position of our bodies. If you do yoga, you know how much better you can think and feel after hanging upside down or changing the rhythm of your breathing. You can use the same idea to recharge in the middle of a strenuous task, and so can everyone in the company.

(1) Take mini-breaks. This is good for longer tasks that require creativity or intense concentration. If you have trouble getting into "flow zone," try going in short spurts; for example, focus for fifty minutes, then relax for ten. Sometimes we do this without realizing it. Your midmorning trips to the coffee machine or midafternoon snack attacks could be your body's code for "I need a break."

(2) Take your eyes off the computer screen. Just as our bodies are built for different kinds of movement, our eyes are built for all different ranges of vision. Favoring close-range tasks, like reading and working on the computer, ruins the eyesight. The best way to protect your eyes is to shift the focus from the screen to a distant object at least every twenty minutes. Fog Creek software, a Silicone Valley graduate with plush new offices in Manhattan, gives every developer a window office. The idea is to periodically look away from your "all-you-can-eat" 30-inch monitors and enjoy the cityscape.

(3) **If you are sitting, stand up.** You can do this without interrupting whatever it is you are doing. In December of last year, my accountant told me I had a few extra thousand dollars to spend on business before the year-end. I decided to upgrade my office, and bought a thing called Nextdesk. It was a lot more expensive than my "last" desk because it had a motor, and it could raise itself up to a standing height and lower itself back to sitting.

(4) **Go for a walk.** When you are ready for a longer break, walking outside accomplishes everything we've talked about, plus it gets you to move and breathe.

People forget how to take breaks and vacations. What if workaholic tendencies persist at your company despite all of your positive role-modeling? A good company will give people plenty of opportunities to unwind. A great company will sometimes step in and enforce the time off, when it sees employees running on empty.

Cinnamon used to shut down A19 over Christmas for two weeks of paid vacation for everyone. That was the only way she could get her employees to take a vacation. She'd also give them long weekends in the summer.

In 2014, Google's Laszlo Bock reported in *Harvard Business Review* that 69 percent of Google employees couldn't stop thinking about work when they went home—and that most of them would like to learn to do that. Then the Dublin office came up with "Dublin Goes Dark"—they just took people's phones and tablets away before sending them home for the night. The Dublin Googlers, temporarily liberated from Gmail and Google Docs, breathed a collective sigh of relief.

Our mental habits are our biggest obstacle to breaking away from the grind. In 2007, Google invited Jon Kabat-Zinn, the author of *Full Catastrophe Living* and *Wherever You Go, There You Are*, to give a lecture on mindfulness. In a 72-minute talk (you can still find it on YouTube), Dr. Kabat-Zinn gave a roomful of very smart-looking people a tour of their own minds—often stuck in *"the story of me."* Then, he led a short meditation to help them *"come to their senses."*

Meditation is more than a short break from anxiety-inducing thinking—although that in itself is no small feat. Dr. Kabat-Zinn called meditation *"tuning your instrument."* He said that many of his meditation students were Nobel Prize laureates who discovered that their best ideas came from *"beyond thinking."*

"It's not what you know. It's what you are willing to learn that you don't know." Mindfulness is *"not second order fluff,"* he concluded, *"but absolutely fundamental to the working order of the business."*

He now has many more followers than detractors. *"For many years the way I thought that I would get everything done was to get less sleep,"* says COO of Facebook Sheryl Sandberg. Not only does she sleep more now, but she also tries to spend at least five minutes a day meditating, even though *"it's really hard."*[55]

CHAPTER 25

LET THE WALLS HELP

> ❝ Cubicle Farm: Monotonous office environment characterized by white collar slaves wasting their lives in pseudo-offices with four foot walls while slowly morphing into zombies. ❞
> — URBANDICTIONARY.COM

> ❝ Ninety-five percent of my assets drive out of the gate every evening. It's my job to maintain a work environment that keeps those people coming back every morning. ❞
> — JIM GOODNIGHT, Founder and CEO, SAS

This is the twenty-first century. Cool companies don't stuff employees in man-cages. And cool up-and-comers don't stick it to the common herd with corner offices, mahogany desks, and personal parking spaces.

Really? What's changed?

Well, it's not just about the war on talent—although cool perks do add up to word-of-mouth recruiting. The more companies rely on employees to innovate, engage customers, and lead and inspire other employees, the more they must pay attention to the environment in which all these activities take place.

Will your people be generous and supportive towards customers and teammates when the office décor shouts scarcity and competition? Right. Hence the definitive move towards abundance, egalitarianism, and shared space.

Not that you shouldn't practice it for its own sake, but generosity towards employees is a time-honored business strategy. It has paid off in a big way at companies like Xerox PARC in the '70s, SAS and Patagonia in the '80s, and our own generation of outliers.

SAS has chosen to remain private just so it could continue to invest in its workforce, hiring when others lay off and adding perks when others take them away. No wonder SAS employee loyalty is legendary. The annual turnover is only 2–3 percent compared to an industry average of twenty-two percent.[56]

Google, LinkedIn, and Facebook have all followed suit in creating office space utopia for their employees. But why stop at the office? Zappos is spending $350 million to develop the entire neighborhood in downtown Las Vegas. Aside from the corporate headquarters, the Downtown Project includes apartment buildings, restaurants, day care, a medical center, outdoor concert space, shops, yoga studios, a dog park, and even office space for other companies, to attract investors and revitalize the area.

The old-school employee-friendly companies focus on tangible benefits, like on-site healthcare, day care, gyms, and free food. However, the newest trend is to pay equal attention to form and substance—especially if you are banking on the creative energies of your staff. Creativity in, creativity out, so to speak. Designer office space is on the rise. And, ever since Apple calligraphed its fonts, no part of office life is exempt from the creative touch.

Just like the Apple products, the best twenty-first-century offices are designed around the user. They shock our twentieth-century eyes because they are actually attractive to humans, not simply convenient for storing paperwork and office machinery. They may resemble living rooms, museums, restaurants, theme parks ... anything but a typical office.

Far from being merely tolerated in exchange for salary and benefits, these offices look like someplace you'd have to pay to get in. Can most companies even afford this kind of space?

Creative doesn't always mean extravagant. Pallotta Teamworks in Los Angeles was built on a budget. The architects, Clive Wilkinson, used shipping containers to section the space into air-conditioned "breathing islands," cutting down the energy usage in the building. Prohibitive cost is not a requirement for creating employee-centered workspaces, even if magazine spreads do favor the high-end. But here's what you *are* likely to find in real life.

COLOR AND TEXTURE

A typical office would be a horrible place for a newborn. Babies' brains need bright colors, fun shapes and new textures to develop. Adult brains need some of that, too. Award-winning office space may lean towards either stimulating or relaxing, but boring and depressing—not so much.

SPACE

Here, too, is something native to man. Whether we were raised in a castle, or a love-shack, we all seem to prefer high ceilings to low, and open spaces to claustrophobic partitions. We also like personal space, which is probably why whoever invented the cubicle thought it was a good idea. Unfortunately, the cubicle rarely feels like personal space, no matter how many pictures of kids and pets we bring inside.

Different employers solve this problem differently. Some give everyone an office with a door. Some have two or three people share an office. Some keep empty offices and small conference rooms first-come-first-served. The new trend, if you are going to have brick and mortar office space, is to fill it with all manner of nooks and crannies for employees to hole up with their laptops. And then, of course, there is my personal favorite: work from home.

NATURAL SUNLIGHT

Fluorescent light is an offense to the eye, while natural sunlight is necessary for every living cell on the planet. And yet, plenty of offices have no windows. If this is your case, you probably save on window-washers, but imagine what it's doing to your people, who toil year after year in a place that would fail PETA requirements.

ECO-FRIENDLINESS

Many employee-friendly features, like fresh air, sunlight, roof gardens, and non-toxic materials, double up as "green." Even though some cost more upfront, green features pay for themselves in the long run—in more ways than one. U.S. Green Building Council reports that green office buildings can increase employee productivity by an average of 16 percent.[57]

DPR Construction (no. 10 on *Fortune's* "100 Best Companies to Work For" in 2014) specializes in green design. Not only the company itself, but many of its clients, like Facebook and Genentech, are known as great places to work. DPR owns two net-zero-energy solar-powered office buildings, in Phoenix and San Diego. The regional headquarters in San Diego houses about sixty employees and an office wine bar. The building boasts minimal interior walls (no cubicle farms here, thank you!), 14-foot exposed ceilings, operable windows, and "Solatube" skylights. In the lobby, a giant digital dashboard continuously tracks energy usage. The construction is expected to pay for itself in a few years in energy savings alone.

Since moving into the new building in 2010, the company has reported reduced absenteeism and increased employee loyalty. An independent survey showed DPR employees to be nearly 100 percent satisfied with the air quality, thermal comfort and personal workspace—well above national averages.

NATURE

All nature in its undisturbed state calms the eye and relaxes the mind. Some companies bring nature into the office in the form of potted plants, aquariums and winter gardens. Others go as far as taking their offices into nature. The Swedish Internet provider White Mountain is situated one hundred feet below ground. The cavernous office space is full of exposed rock. Sunlight comes in through a glass opening in the ceiling.

Then there is Selgas Cano, a Spanish architectural firm that's built its glass-covered studio right in the woods of Madrid. On first thought, this might strike you as an odd choice. Wouldn't you rather have your office next to a Starbucks? But if you've ever tried to breathe in Madrid, you'd know that the architects have their priorities straight: oxygen above all.

FOOD

Feeding the mind and the senses is important, but let's not forget our stomachs. Google has a rule that no employee be more than one hundred meters away from food. In addition to free cafeterias, Google offices sneak in fully stocked kitchens around every corner.

NAPPING

Since we are talking about everything people need for healthy work and an occasional break, what about sleep? Sometimes taking a nap is by far the most productive thing you can do for yourself and the company.

When venture capitalist and entrepreneur Rich Stromback goes to the World Economic Forum in Davos, he naps every day between the hours of 4:00 and 8:00 p.m. *"It's the most efficient time to catch up on sleep, so I can be fresh when the moment is opportune."*[58]

Stromback can go back to his hotel room to get a nap in-between networking sessions. But what about a typical employee trapped in the office? A few companies have started quiet rooms with hammocks, lounge chairs, and other such necessary equipment. Google employees can use a napping pod—a recliner with a soundproof dome covering the head and upper body. Hearst, *Newsweek,* and Time Warner send their employees to Yelo, a napping spa in midtown Manhattan.

If you can't give your employees a comfortable place to nap, the least you can do is take away the shame. Dozing off in a meeting is awkward, but there is no reason why one of your devoted servants couldn't take a short nap at his desk. This is not just my opinion. Apparently, the Japanese have been doing it even longer than Google.

Inemuri is the Japanese practice of sleeping on the job. It literally means, "sleeping while present." It is a way for an employee to show how committed they are to working. In other words, the employee spends so much time working that they sleep too little at home and have to do inemuri. Some people even fake inemuri, so that their bosses believe they are working hard.[59]

Okay, so faking a nap won't earn you a quick promotion this side of the Pacific. But neither will faking work when your brain is flashing red. Western science concurs: it's better to put off important tasks until you're refreshed.

Tests by NASA have concluded that napping during the day can improve working memory (i.e. focusing attention on one task while holding other tasks in memory) a fundamental ability critical to performing complex work.[60]

ONE-OF-A-KIND FEATURES

Your employees are not just people. They are a special kind of people. They care about your business enough to create something new or help others. The more they are able to express themselves at work, the more distinct your products and services. This is where the walls can truly help. Give people a shared space that speaks to them in some remarkable way. Forget about impressing outsiders. Give your people an *inside* view of *their* business and *their* cause.

Red Bull's London office has a reception area that turns into a bar at night. I am rapidly approaching the age when I'd rather go to bed early than stay after work and party with the receptionist, but I can see how a Red-Bullish person would be all over this idea.

And here's Facebook's Ben Barry:

> *We had lived in our previous building for several years, and it had accumulated all this cool stuff. And as we moved into this place we, as a company, collectively freaked out a bit. All these white walls—it felt wrong. But it was really important to me for it not to be done for people. They needed to take ownership and initiative to own their environment. Because I believe that when people have control over their physical space, it empowers them to take more risks in product development.*[61]

SLIDES

No, not the PowerPoint kind. Adult-size stainless and painted steel, straight, spiral, and custom-built slides for employees who prefer neither elevator nor the stairs. There is something irresistible about giant slides mixed in with glass doors and conference tables. If you disagree, you might change your mind after visiting Massey and Harris, a *"playground solutions"* provider that carries office slides:

> *Four of the top ten coolest places to work in the UK have slides in their offices. Google, Lego, Red Bull and others have all installed slides in various guises to bring a smile to the faces of the staff. Ticketmaster, Liftshare.com and Cossatto all have*

slides installed in their offices ... and the red spiral slide manufactured for the Virgin Media stands at the Ideal Homes exhibition. Fully bespoke with a range of additional options, the slides ordered have been straight, curved, extra steep and ended up coming out of walls into reception areas. We provide initial design concept drawings and supply full working drawings once the design has been signed off. [62]

If you can't yet afford your dream office, start small. You can work your way up to the five-story atrium with a three-story slide, like the one at Corus Quay in Toronto. It's really the thought that counts, anyway. Once your employees get it that the company is looking out for their comfort, your purpose is mostly achieved, and the rest is just icing.

SAS started in 1976 with fresh fruit and free M&Ms. In 1980, the company broke ground at its current headquarters and added on-site day care. In 1984 came the fitness center, medical center and a café.

When designing its office space, Patagonia focused on the essentials. Communication, healthy food, and family, not necessarily in that order:

Since 1984 we have had no private offices, an architectural arrangement that sometimes creates distractions but also helps keep communication open. That year we opened a cafeteria where employees can gather throughout the day that to this day serves healthy, mostly vegetarian food. And we also opened, at Malinda Chouinard's insistence, an on-site child care center, at the time one of only 150 in the country (today there are more than 3,000). The presence of children playing in the yard, or having lunch with their parents in the cafeteria helps keep the company atmosphere more familial than corporate. We also continue to offer—mostly for the benefit of working parents but also for others—flexible working hours and job sharing.[63]

In 2013, the *Boston Globe* interviewed HR execs of four up-and-coming Boston tech firms: Raj Aggarwal of Localytics, Jim Gemmell of Akamai, Leslie Brunner of Athenahealth, and James Kizielewicz of Kronos. Nothing over the top here, just simple things that matter to employees:

GLOBE: So, what's your favorite perk that other companies don't offer?

BRUNNER: We have a lot of free stuff: food, beer, swag. People love it ...

KIZIELEWICZ: ... We had these crappy basketball nets outside in the parking lot. Guys would go out there and play, and they said, "These things stink." So, boom, now we have NBA-quality glass backboards. We've tripled the number of people who play basketball out there.

GEMMELL: We do some fun things locally. Right out in the middle of Kendall, we'll have a barbecue. It's just a great way for people to come together.

AGGARWAL: A real focus on great craft beers. There's a rotating supply, they go pretty quickly, but we've got a few really passionate beer guys in the company. They're selecting, they're doing polls, and everyone is looking forward to what it will be. We've got two taps, and so there's always something a little lighter and something a little darker.[64]

Making employees feel at home is easy if you try. But it's just as easy to make them feel like wards of a Russian state-run orphanage. Try these timeless classics: (1) dirty bathrooms; (2) no refrigerator space for employee lunches; (3) no assigned desk, start your new hire on someone else's desk; (4) shortage of office supplies; (5) clutter; and (6) if you have an office in India, try opening it in a residential area.

That last one is from Axero's live-and-learn files. Once upon a time, we thought a quiet neighborhood off the beaten track would be a perk. But we forgot to ask our employees. Apparently, we were not the quirky and cool company we thought we were. We were losers who couldn't afford prime office space downtown. Our poor public image reflected on anyone desperate enough to join our company—even if they weren't required to come to the office.

Bringing the right stuff into the office puts a smile on people's faces. But, so does taking the wrong stuff out.

A long time ago, I saw Beauty Co. move its IT staff into a newly renovated space. It had large windows, and it was airy and well-lit. First, they filled it with wall-to-wall cubicles. Then they mounted open shelves on top of the partitions. Within hours of moving in, people filled the overhead storage with assorted rubbish. Once an item made it all the way up there, it never came down. It just sat there collecting dust and obstructing the view. It was sad to see all this money and effort spent to make a perfectly good space completely uninhabitable.

Keep your furniture away from the windows. Lower the partitions, so people can see the daylight. Get rid of the fluorescent lights. Ask people to sort through the clutter, and don't design junk-piling into the floor plan.

Use your office space efficiently. Customize every square foot. Do you really need a reception desk? (I am not saying you don't. But it's a question worth asking.) When I came to HubSpot, I was greeted by a blackboard with some random thoughts and drawings in color chalk. I took out my cell phone and announced myself to my host, who came out right away and gave me a tour. That was as good of a first impression as any, and to this day I have a strong preference for black chalkboards over white dry-erase ones.

You might decide, as we have, to get rid of the office altogether. We have Communifire—but a face-to-face collaborative space is important. And there is plenty of it in San Diego. My favorite is The Living Room in La Jolla. It has the best view of the ocean, and the hookah bar upstairs is usually empty during the day.

CHAPTER 26

PLAY

> ❝ If what you've done is stupid but it works, then it really isn't that stupid at all. ❞
>
> — DAVID LETTERMAN

> ❝ Here's to the crazy ones. ❞
>
> — Apple, "Think Different" ad campaign, 1997

I was pacing up and down my living room, ignoring the sitcom I had turned on to help myself unwind. The following day *Inc.* magazine was going to interview me about the Millennials, and I was nervous. I felt like I was in one of those dreams where you are suddenly back in high school, and there's a test you didn't study for. I must have looked pitiful to my girlfriend Kimberly, because she decided to give me a pep talk.

> KIMBERLY: What are you worried about, Tim? What's the worst that can happen?
> TIM: I could make a fool out of myself.
> KIMBERLY: Maybe that's the best that can happen! Aren't they sick of business people all saying the same thing all the time?

Was she right? What if being a fool was okay, but being stiff, boring and predictable was a waste of their time and mine? And what if she wasn't just talking about the interview?

Of the dozens of companies I've worked for in my teens and twenties, only one is a name you would recognize. It was also hands-down the most fun I've ever had on a job. Was that just a coincidence? Or is outrageous fun somehow connected to extraordinary performance? Those of you who have never worked for a mega-successful, fast-growing best-in-class company, hold on, don't answer just yet. Those of you who have, did you see a connection?

This particular employer was a chain of restaurants known more for their ambience than their food. Once I started there as a waiter, I got in on many of their secrets. It was certainly an unusual place to work.

For starters, why were employees leaving a single-toilet bathroom in small groups? This mystery was revealed a few days later, after I had smoked my first joint in the employee bathroom. It also partially explained mystery no. 2: how did a handful of overworked, undertrained employees handle a full restaurant plus a line at the door? On the weekends, we'd have ten tables each, usually four to ten customers to a table. That's fifty or sixty hungry, thirsty, and alcohol-deprived souls depending on you to satisfy their various unmet needs, all at once.

How did we do it? Pot certainly helped to ease the pressure. Another trick was that you didn't mind the customers so much if you got wasted with them, and even ahead of them. Free alcohol was not in the employee handbook, so here's what you did. You went up to the bar and ordered a drink for yourself, as if a customer had ordered it. Then you came back and said that the customer didn't like it and put in the real order. As long as you did your job well, no one questioned why your customers were always so fussy about the drinks. Meanwhile, I'm guessing that corporate made an allowance for "employee theft," and everything checked and balanced.

Once you started running around with a few drinks in you, your hormones kicked in. Where were the napping pods when I was young? In contrast to modern-day Googlers, we were low-tech unspoiled folk. Our natural urges required no special accommodations. We were willing to have sex anywhere—the bathrooms, the walk-in freezer, or out by the trash bins, weather permitting.

You could say that we lived by our own version of the immortal in-flight emergency mask drill: Take care of yourself before assisting others. As long as we were in a good mood ourselves, it was all fun and games with the customers. The less serious you were, the better the tips.

There were tricks to having the whole table in stitches. Like how do you work an all-guy or an all-girl table? Hint: not in the same way. If you wanted the dudes to leave you a decent tip, you had to play up to them. Be brash, so you wouldn't come across as a pansy male waiter. If you went too far, you'd bring them a round of free beers to settle the score.

With the girls, you wanted to be subtle. No mean jokes, just playful ones. Like pointing to your front teeth after they had eaten their salads, pretending they had a piece of lettuce stuck in-between. Watch them freak out and pull out their pocket mirrors. Then give them the "you got it" and say something nice. Sit or kneel at the table to "turn on the heat." Thumb-wrestle them, or guess what they are about to order. If you hit the mood just right, you made good money.

With all the chemicals rushing through our bodies, our focus suffered a bit, and spills were a nightly event. If you dropped a T-bone steak on the floor, the whole kitchen would scream "5-second rule!!" before throwing the steak into the deep fryer for a few seconds to sanitize it. Fortunately, the customers were not there to see it. So, when you asked them how the steak was, they'd say it was the best they'd ever had, and you'd be too drunk to feel any remorse. Hell, some nights by the closing time, we were too drunk to walk!

Are you sure you are not telling me a fish story, Tim? Where was management in all of this? There must have been at least one adult in charge of your cuckoo's nest!

Yes, we had managers. To their infinite credit, our managers knew a good thing when they saw it, and learned to make themselves invisible. After we'd memorized the menus, we were pretty much on our own. When I did need a manager, say, to void an item, he would materialize and take care of the void. Then he would do the best Homer Simpson laugh I've ever heard and disappear before I had a chance to thank him. I had nothing but admiration and respect for the guy!

I am sorry, Tim, no employer in his right mind would leave a bunch of crazy drunken kids in charge of his business. Else, he would be asking for a nasty lawsuit. And that's just the best-case scenario. Worst case—the whole restaurant burns down.

Nope. Nothing like that happened, at least while I was there. On the contrary, night after night went by without a hiccup. Customers returned. And the business grew by leaps and bounds. We served the same food as other restaurants. We had the same tables and chairs. It was the craziness that gave us our competitive edge. And if the adults in charge wanted full shareholder value, they had to release us from our straitjackets.

In 2008 recession hit, and most mid-priced restaurants lost customers. The downward trend continued for several years, except for a small group of restaurants featuring young waitresses in skimpy uniforms emphasizing cleavage. Twin Peaks, Canz, and Tilted Kilt all posted growth of 30 percent or higher in 2011. In 2012, Bikinis Sports Bar & Grill successfully registered the term "breastaurant" as a trademark with the United States Patent and Trademark Office.

Hooters, the author of the original concept, objected to being called a breastaurant. It slumped with the rest of the industry, as it tried to clean up its public image. Meanwhile, its thriving competitors fully embraced theirs. *"We believe in feeding the ego before feeding the stomach,"* says Twin Peaks owner Randy DeWitt. *"We hire only spectacular talent,"* confides Rod Lynch, the owner of Tilted Kilt.[65]

We often make assumptions about what makes people and companies successful. Our assumptions have more to do with our own insecurities than with any hard facts. Consequently, almost everyone points to hard work as a success factor, and completely ignores easy fun.

But fun is essential. Google, Zappos, LinkedIn, Camden Trust, and many other top companies believe that goofing off regularly amounts to a strategic advantage in the marketplace. I don't have any stats on this, but intuitively it makes sense. When do your best ideas come to you? When you stare at your computer? When you are in a meeting? Or when you are taking a shower, out for a jog, or joking with friends?

Zappos holds annual Bald and Blue days, when employees can shave their heads or dye their hair blue. The company will contribute between $50 and $300 to local charities on behalf of every participant. CEO Tony Hsieh owns a fleet of party buses, a party house, and a 40-foot-long praying mantis that shoots fire from its antennas, mounted on a truck. The buses and the house are available to employees and business associates for spur-of-the-moment trips and parties. They are essential to Zappos' corporate goal to *"create fun and a little weirdness."* And the mantis is a reminder of the scale on which the fun and creativity take place.

All of that aside, fun at work doesn't need to be outrageous, nor should it be confined to after-hours. Google combines groundbreaking software development with scooter parking stalls, whimsical doodles, and public April Fool's Day jokes.[66] HubSpot offers a jam room full of musical equipment, just in case employees need to get over a mental block or simply relax. LinkedIn and other tech companies hold hackdays, so people can take a break from assigned projects and play with products and design features of their choice.

We could all stand a little less stress and a little more fun at work. But here's the catch. Fun can't be scheduled, developed, or implemented. Constructive and productive fun at work cannot be achieved by any of the fun-sucking methods proliferating in the business world. Nor is it necessary. Your people already know how to have fun. Not like they do it at Google or Zappos, but their own brand of fun. The management's job is simply to allow it. Let the people have a ball and let yourself be ridiculous. You already are, by the way. All there is to do is to embrace it.

Hence the genius of my restaurant managers: they taught us to laugh in the face of a stressful job, and then they got out of the way and let us run with it. Do you think a lighter touch could solve a problem or two at your company? How about these two:

Job Title	Biggest Challenge at Work
Collection Supervisor	*"Dealing with negativity"*
Head of Programmes	*"Enthusiasm"*

A well-executed Homer Simpson laugh can diffuse a lot of negativity, even from people who can't pay their bills. (What else have you got to say to them, anyway?) As for enthusiasm, if you heard my old manager do it, you'd immediately stand up and cheer.

Besides relieving stress and breaking up the routine, eccentric jokes serve a business purpose. The famous advertising executive David Ogilvy said, *"The best ideas come as jokes. Make your thinking as funny as possible."* And here's a story about that.

Newman's Own line of natural and organic foods started as a joke between actor, Paul Newman, and his friend, author A.E. Hotchner. The two used to pour Paul's homemade salad dressing into fancy wine bottles and give as gifts to family and friends. When someone jokingly suggested they sell it in stores, Paul proposed to "shamelessly exploit his celebrity status" by putting his face on the label—but only if all of the profits went to charity.

The first Newman's Own salad dressing appeared in stores in 1982, taglined: *Fine Foods Since February.* Since then, the company has donated over $400 million to charities and First Amendment awards.

In 1988, Paul Newman co-founded Association of Hole in the Wall Camps, residential summer camps for seriously ill children. Today SeriousFun Children's Network operates in fifty countries and has hosted more than 385,000 children free of charge. Newman's Own has also sponsored the *New York Times* Neediest Cases Fund, Shining Hope for Communities, Safe Water Network, Edible Schoolyard NYC, Fisher House Foundation, the WILD Young Women Programme (New Zealand), and Pilgrims Hospices (UK). They are able to make all this money and solve all these problems, without thinking of themselves as a straitlaced serious business, and, largely, because of that very fact.

"Play" is the last piece of advice in this book. I put it last because I wanted you to learn all the other principles first. Many companies try to force "fun" on their disgruntled, micromanaged, and slave-driven employees. It always backfires, because fun is about self-expression. And to express yourself, you need to feel safe first and trust those around you. It's about the company and the people looking out for one another, instead of each protecting one's own turf.

All the preceding chapters help you build precisely this kind of a workplace, from the ground up. The real work within any work we do is to overcome old habits that obstruct our relationships with each other and with our better selves. Once the lessons in these chapters become your company's second nature, all there's left to do is ... play.

AFTERWORD

Hello again!

I picture you taking your eyes off the last page of this book. The whirlwind tour of companies, personalities, accomplishments and ideas has just ended. Welcome back to yourself! I bet you feel good. And I envy you a bit.

Finishing a book is always a favorite moment for me. There's a sense of accomplishment. Needless to say, I don't finish every book I read. I don't even start reading many good books, even though they sound like a well of wisdom and a treasure trove of opportunity. I just never get to it. So, whenever I finish one, it's an event. But there's more.

I remember finishing *The 4-Hour Workweek* by Tim Ferris. I was on the plane from Philly to San Diego. (If I finish a book, it's probably going to be on that 6-hour flight which I take every year, after spending a week with my family.) I put down my iPad and sat back in my chair.

I had a really good feeling about it. A surge of hope, mixed with anticipation—and I was taking it in. I wasn't imagining myself working 4-hour weeks or anything like that. I enjoyed my work. But I was building a company, so I was responsible for other people's workweeks. Our customers relied on us to work smart. And our competitors were breathing down our necks.

I noticed that Tim Ferris and I had a lot in common. We were both efficiency nazis. I didn't just agree with his ideas, I was already practicing many of them. I also noticed how much I was missing. At the time, I was struggling with the whole idea of delegating my best skills. Vivek and I had just cut loose three-quarters of our developers and rewritten a ton of code that wasn't up to our standards. We were at the right place at the right time. But the growth wasn't happening, because ... well, maybe I had just figured it out!

I remember thinking, "Now that I've read the book, what can I do differently?" The change had to be small enough, not to overwhelm our already strained capacity. Yet it had to have an impact—to prove that I was moving the company in the right direction.

I felt burned by the whole outsourcing fiasco. But the idea that someone as demanding as myself—Tim Ferris—had succeeded at it gave me the comfort to try again. I took his advice and focused on clarity. Get as detailed as I can about the outcome I want, and leave the "how" entirely to the employee.

And that was "how" Axero turned the corner from a startup to a growing company. We took a small, tiny leap of faith and perfected it until it didn't hurt anymore. It became our way and it still is today.

Do you remember the 5-15 report from Chapter 19, *Give Them a Voice?* When I learned about it, I thought it was harmless enough for us to try. This was about a year ago, as I was wrapping up *Who the Hell Wants to Work for You?* It appealed to me, because I still wasn't sure we were going about our jobs in the best possible way. So, I just asked everyone to start doing 5-15s and sending them up the chain. At first, I noticed that people liked writing and reading these reports. But looking back, I am amazed at the difference they've made for us.

First, everyone knows what everyone else is working on, and it's a good thing. People appreciate each other and don't act like they are the only ones doing anything useful. Second, everyone knows what's important to everyone else. Since sales and customer service people share their reports, we all know what's important to prospects and customers. We prioritize accordingly. Third, we set realistic goals, since we understand our capacity and priorities much better. Fourth, since we set realistic goals and are totally transparent, everyone fully owns his job. People not only deliver superior results, but they are constantly improving the process, so that a new person can eventually step in their shoes and replace them, as they move up in the company onto bigger things. This is exactly what we need to keep growing!

I don't know which of the many practices in this book will become your tiny leap of faith. But I do know there is at least one that will work for you. The one you are ready to take on this very moment. And I am excited for you!

Tim Eisenhauer
San Diego, California
November 5, 2016

ABOUT THE AUTHOR

WHO THE HELL IS TIM EISENHAUER?

The thing to know about me is that I care about employee engagement the way environmentalists care about clean air and patients care about curing disease. One obvious reason is that I run a virtual company in a highly competitive market. If people aren't psyched to work for me, we go out of business tomorrow. But, as any motivational psychologist will tell you, practical considerations are rarely the ultimate driver. The real reason is personal.

In 1999 I stopped playing college basketball and gave up the idea of becoming a pro athlete. Up to that point, all of what you'd call my career happened on the basketball court. I didn't have a résumé. I wasn't getting paid. I played because I wanted to play.

I had the most miserable time switching careers. My adrenaline-starved brain kept searching for "the game." I was dropping in and out of schools, changing majors, quitting jobs, and starting businesses.

In 2008 Vivek Thakur and I co-founded Axero Solutions. Little by little, through trial and error, our company became the no-bull game zone for us and our employees. That happened first. Everything else came later. Our first successful product. Big-name customers. Steady cash.

In 2014, I started covering employee engagement on the Axero blog. It quickly became one of the main reasons people read my blog. Later that year, I published an eBook, *22 Surefire Ways to Boost Employee Engagement.* The number of downloads shocked me. I wanted to know why people from all over the world were looking for employee engagement advice. Every time somebody downloaded my eBook, I asked them about their biggest challenge at work.

I noticed that people were looking to employee engagement to solve all kinds of challenges. The only problem was nobody knew where to find it. This is the reason my humble eBook attracts so many readers: people are hungry for ideas! Tying employee engagement to common-sense workplace principles gives them a place to start.

I used the twenty-two principles from the eBook and added one more—*Give Them a Break*—to write the book you've just read. And I can't wait to hear from you. What is your biggest challenge at work? Did this book help you solve it?

FURTHER READING (AND WRITING)

Not a day that goes by that I don't learn something new about managing people. I learn from my job, from my research, and from all the people who keep sending me their challenges. To read all the stories, commentary and advice, join my email list. It currently has nearly thirty thousand subscribers.

Sign up now at http://timeisenhauer.com/newsletter

Of course, I am not the only manager trying to get better at what I do. We all are. Connect with me and other managers at timeisenhauer.com. Weigh in on their challenges. And tell us about yours. I look forward to seeing you there!

ACKNOWLEDGEMENTS

The process of writing and publishing this book turned out to be much more work than I expected. Had I known then what it would take to publish a book, I probably wouldn't have done it.

Writing the book was the easy part. Everything that came after was a whole new way of doing things. What a journey.

First, I'd like to thank all the agents that turned me away, didn't reply, or tried to get *me* to pay *them* to represent me. Publishing the book on my own was a good choice.

Second, I was lucky to have people around me to help keep me motivated to turn this book into reality.

Olga Cannistraro, thank you for everything. The countless hours spent talking through things on the phone, researching, writing, editing, planning, and thinking. This book wouldn't exist without you. Thank you.

To Ann Maynard, my editor, thank you for your guidance, and for tightening things up, helping to cut the fat, and for fixing the structure.

Vivek Thakur, thank you for ten amazing years of friendship. Building Axero together has been and continues to be one of the most rewarding things I've ever done in life. Having you on my side makes it so much better.

To my parents, Ike and Susie Eisenhauer, thank you for bringing me into this world, getting me involved in all kinds of activities when I was a kid, and for making sure that I got a good education. I owe everything to you both. Mom, thank you for finally reading a non-fiction book. And when I was considering changing the title, thanks for encouraging me to keep it.

Maggie, Silas, and Ani—thanks for reminding me of the things that really matter in life.

To my brother, Trevor Eisenhauer, thanks for being the best brother anyone could ever ask for—and for all the time you helped editing, proofreading, designing, layout, and everything else. It's been a blessing to be able to work with you side-by-side.

I'd like to thank everyone at Beauty Co. for giving a clueless intern a chance to figure out what he *didn't* want to do in life. Thank you for making me pull hair out of computers and wipe hard drives in "the cage." Thank you for making me walk around the office and run unnecessary updates. Thank you for making me drive hundreds of miles to fix non-existing problems. And thank you for firing me.

Thank you to all the people and organizations mentioned in this book. You inspire me beyond what words can even explain. You've given me faith that work can, and should, be fun and meaningful.

Several people helped greatly by discussing, reviewing, and providing feedback on my research and drafts of the book, including Brian Teel, Kimberly St. John, Siah Dowlatshawhi, David Grishaver, Patsy Reves Earl, John Earl, Rebecca Verhoef, Chris Johnson, Doug Watson, Sammy Tovar, Ryan Holiday, Mervyn Friedlander, Raja Sandhu, Jaspreet Kaur, Bryce Johannes, Nick Geczi, Matt Trujillo, Atul Ahuja, Raghav Khunger, John Fike, Jessica Mehring, Devin DiGonno, Chuck Vigeant, Emily James,

Aaron James, Vanessa Merten, Rob Merten, Lea Bays, Harper Steele, Kelly Parkinson, and everyone at 1106 Design.

Finally, to my readers. I hope this book makes a difference in your life and your work. Thank you for reading it.

ENDNOTES

1 Swanson, D. JoAnne. "What I Learned When I Quit My Job: Part One." Rethinking the Job Culture. 2004. Accessed July 14, 2016. https://radicalunjobbing.wordpress.com/2010/06/30/what-i-learned-when-i-quit-my-job-part-one/.

2 Belfort, Jordan. *The Wolf of Wall Street*. New York, NY: Bantam, 2007. Print.

3 Benedictus, Leo. "Want to Work for Google? Answer These Five Questions." *The Guardian,* February 24, 2014. Accessed July 14, 2016. https://www.theguardian.com/technology/shortcuts/2014/feb/24/work-for-google-five-questions-laszlo-bock.

4 Nisen, Max. "Tony Hsieh's Brilliant Strategy For Hiring Kind People." *Business Insider,* November 22, 2013. Accessed July 14, 2016. http://www.businessinsider.com/tony-hsieh-zappos-hiring-strategy-2013-11.

5 Taylor, Bill. "Hire for Attitude, Train for Skill." *Harvard Business Review,* February 1, 2011. Accessed July 14, 2016. https://hbr.org/2011/02/hire-for-attitude-train-for-sk/.

6 Friedman, Thomas L. "How to Get a Job at Google." *The New York Times,* February 22, 2014. Accessed July 14, 2016. http://www.nytimes.com/2014/02/23/opinion/sunday/friedman-how-to-get-a-job-at-google.html?_r=0.

[7] Silverman, Rachel Emma. "Companies Try to Make the First Day for New Hires More Fun." *The Wall Street Journal.* May 28, 2013. http://www.wsj.com/articles/SB1000142412788732 3336104578501631475934850.

[8] Markelz, Michelle. "Trash the Ratings." *Profile,* 2014. http://profilemagazine.com/2013/motorola-solutions-2/.

[9] Dishman, Lydia. "A Simple, Science-Backed Way To Solve The Employee-Engagement Problem." *Fast Company,* October 8, 2013. Accessed July 14, 2016. http://www.fastcompany.com/3019508/work-smart/a-simple-science-backed-way-to-solve-the-employee-engagement-problem.

[10] Dishman, Lydia. "A Simple, Science-Backed Way To Solve The Employee-Engagement Problem." *Fast Company,* October 8, 2013. Accessed July 14, 2016. http://www.fastcompany.com/3019508/work-smart/a-simple-science-backed-way-to-solve-the-employee-engagement-problem.

[11] Eisenhauer, Tim. "Case Study: How Best Collateral Turned Document Sharing Into an Engagement Engine for 75 Employees." Axero Solutions Blog, Fall 2015. https://axerosolutions.com/blogs/timeisenhauer/pulse/308/case-study-how-best-collateral-turned-document-sharing-into-an-engagement-engine-for-75-employees.

[12] Nayar, Vineet. "Managing 3 Types of Bad Bosses." *Harvard Business Review,* December 1, 2014. https://hbr.org/2014/12/managing-3-types-of-bad-bosses.

[13] Garvin, David A. "How Google Sold Its Engineers on Management." *Harvard Business Review,* December 2013. December 1, 2014. https://hbr.org/2013/12/how-google-sold-its-engineers-on-management.

[14] Garvin, David A. "How Google Sold Its Engineers on Management." *Harvard Business Review,* December 2013. December 1, 2014. https://hbr.org/2013/12/how-google-sold-its-engineers-on-management.

[15] "Learn about Google's Manager Research." Guide: Identify What Makes a Great Manager. https://rework.withgoogle.com guides/managers-identify-what-makes-a-great-manager/steps/ learn-about-googles-manager-research/.

[16] Carlson, Nicholas. "Google Paid This Man $100 Million: Here's His Story." *Business Insider,* April 6, 2013. http://www.business insider.com/neal-mohan-googles-100-million-man-2013-4.

[17] Lizhi, Xu. "I Swallowed a Moon Made of Iron." *The Washington Post.* November 12, 2014 Web.

[18] Jobs, Steve. "Steve Jobs: Stanford Commencement Address." Address, Stanford University, June 12, 2005. June 12, 2005. http://news.stanford.edu/2005/06/14/jobs-061505/.

[19] Schultz, Howard, and Dori Jones Young. *Pour Your Heart Into It: How Starbucks Built a Company One Cup at a Time.* 1st ed. New York, NY: Hachette Books, 1997.

[20] Clayberg, Eric. "How Google Sold Its Engineers on Management." Interview by David A. Garvin. *Harvard Business Review.* December 2013. https://hbr.org/2013/12/how-google-sold-its-engineers-on-management.

[21] Mintzberg, Henry. "Why Don't Managers Coach and Develop Their People?" Interview by Terence R. Traut. Coach Your Employees. November 2007. http://www.coachyouremployees .com/library/Entelechy_speaks_to_Henry_Mintzberg_about_ Coaching.pdf.

[22] Milinovich, John. "How Fast-Growing Startups Can Fix Internal Communication Before It Breaks." First Round Review. Accessed July 14, 2016. http://firstround.com/review/How-Fast-Growing-Startups-Can-Fix-Internal-Communication-Before-It-Breaks/.

[23] Wilkins, Muriel Maignan. "Signs That You're a Micromanager." *Harvard Business Review,* November 11, 2014. https://hbr .org/2014/11/signs-that-youre-a-micromanager.

[24] Wilkins, Muriel Maignan. "Signs That You're a Micromanager." *Harvard Business Review,* November 11, 2014. https://hbr.org/ 2014/11/signs-that-youre-a-micromanager.

[25] Davis, Jim. "How SAS Became The World's Best Place To Work." Interview by Mark C. Crowley. *Fast Company.* January 22, 2013. http://www.fastcompany.com/3004953/ how-sas-became-worlds-best-place-work.

[26] Garvin, David A. "How Google Sold Its Engineers on Management." *Harvard Business Review,* December 2013. December 1, 2014. https://hbr.org/2013/12/how-google-sold-its-engineers-on-management.

[27] Carlson, Nicholas. "Google Paid This Man $100 Million: Here's His Story." *Business Insider,* April 6, 2013. http://www.business insider.com/neal-mohan-googles-100-million-man-2013-4.

[28] Davis, Stephanie. "How Google Sold Its Engineers on Management." Interview by David A. Garvin. *Harvard Business Review.* December 2013. https://hbr.org/2013/12/how-google-sold-its-engineers-on-management.

[29] "The Importance of Being Known: The Positive Impact That Managers Can Have by Becoming Better Known as a Person." BlessingWhite, November 11, 2014. http://blessingwhite.com/

article/2012/08/20/the-importance-of-being-known-the-positive-impact-that-managers-can-have-by-becoming-better-known-as-a-person-2/.

[30] "The Importance of Being Known: The Positive Impact That Managers Can Have by Becoming Better Known as a Person." BlessingWhite, November 11, 2014. http://blessingwhite.com/article/2012/08/20/the-importance-of-being-known-the-positive-impact-that-managers-can-have-by-becoming-better-known-as-a-person-2/.

[31] Stone, Brad. "Why Facebook Needs Sheryl Sandberg." *BloombergBusinessweek,* May 11, 2011. http://www.bloomberg.com/ncws/articles/2011-05-12/why-facebook-needs-sheryl-sandberg.

[32] Hsieh, Tony. *Delivering Happiness: A Path to Profits, Passion, and Purpose.* 1st ed. Grand Central Publishing, 2013.

[33] Schmidt, Eric. "Apple vs Google." Interview by Robert Lane Greene. *Intelligent Life Magazine,* Winter 2010. Eric Schmidt talked about the difference in July when he visited *The Economist* in London.

[34] Kotter, John, and Kotter International. "Does corporate culture drive financial performance?" *Forbes.* February 10, 2011. http://www.forbes.com/sites/johnkotter/2011/02/10/does-corporate-culture-drive-financial-performance/#663618a2672d.

[35] Wilson, Mark. "Meet Ben Barry, Facebook's Minister Of Propaganda." *Fast Company,* CO.Design, November 5, 2012. http://www.fastcodesign.com/1671050/meet-ben-barry-facebooks-minister-of-propaganda.

[36] Davis, Jim. "How SAS Became The World's Best Place To Work." Interview by Mark C. Crowley. *Fast Company.*

January 22, 2013. http://www.fastcompany.com/3004953/how-sas-became-worlds-best-place-work.

[37] Wakabayashi, Daisuke. "Tim Cook's Vision for 'His' Apple Begins to Emerge." *The Wall Street Journal,* July 7, 2014. http://www.wsj.com/articles/tim-cooks-apple-takes-shape-1404757939.

[38] Cook, Tim. Interview by Charlie Rose. "Tim Cook, Who Succeeded Steve Jobs as C.E.O. of Apple in 2011, Talks about the Company's next Chapter and the Release of the Apple Watch." PBS. September 12, 2014.

[39] "What Is the Primary Cause of Negativity in Your Work Place?" About.com, April 2, 2014.

[40] "7 Vital Trends Disrupting Today's Workplace. Results and Data from 2013 TINYpulse Employee Engagement Survey." TINYpulse, 2013. https://www.tinypulse.com/resources/employee-engagement-survey-2013.

[41] Roth, Daniel. "The Monk CEO: How Carlos Ghosn Manages 3 Companies, $140B in Sales and Still Stays Human." LinkedIn, November 5, 2014. https://www.linkedin.com/pulse/20141105133121-29092-the-monk-ceo-how-carlos-ghosn-manages-3-companies-140b-in-sales-and-still-stays-human.

[42] Bock, Laszlo. "Passion, Not Perks Passion, Not Perks." Think with Google, September 2011. https://www.thinkwithgoogle.com/articles/passion-not-perks.html.

[43] Staff, GoodData. "How to Use Yammer to Measure Employee Morale and Sentiment." GoodData, October 4, 2013. http://www.gooddata.com/blog/measure-employee-morale-with-yammer.

[44] Bock, Laszlo. "Google's Scientific Approach to Work-Life Balance (and Much More)." *Harvard Business Review,* March

27, 2014. https://hbr.org/2014/03/googles-scientific-approach-to-work-life-balance-and-much-more/.

[45] "Our culture"—Company—Google
http://www.google.com/about/company/facts/culture/

[46] "Ten things we know to be true"—Company—Google
https://www.google.com/about/company/philosophy/

[47] Patagonia Company Information: "Our Reason for Being"
http://www.patagonia.com/us/patagonia.go?assetid=2047

[48] Patagonia Company Information: "Our Reason for Being"
http://www.patagonia.com/us/patagonia.go?assetid=2047

[49] Hansel, Mark. "Company Shatters Volunteering Record." *The Republic,* August 12, 2014. http://www.therepublic.com/view/local_story/Company-shatters-volunteering-_1407890909.

[50] Kim, Jihoon. "7 Secrets of Google's Epic Organizational Culture." Office Vibe, September 30, 2013. https://www.officevibe.com/blog/7-secrets-of-googles-epic-organizational-culture.

[51] Shropshire, Corilyn. "6 Minutes a Day for Bathroom Breaks? Union Cries Foul." *Chicago Tribune,* July 10, 2014. http://articles.chicagotribune.com/2014-07-10/business/chi-bathroom-breaks-watersavers-union-complaint-20140710_1_bathroom-union-cries-breaks.

[52] Brunner, Leslie. "For Tech Firms, Culture Is King." Interview by Michael Farrel. *Boston Globe.* November 11, 2014. http://archive.boston.com/business/technology/2013/11/17/for-tech-firms-culture-king/C6lxlVEyr4pzqRl5xJe23M/story.html.

[53] Stone, Brad. "Why Facebook Needs Sheryl Sandberg." *BloombergBusinessweek,* May 11, 2011. http://www.bloomberg

.com/news/articles/2011-05-12/why-facebook-needs-sheryl-sandberg.

[54] Adams, Scott. The Joy of Work: *Dilbert's Guide to Finding Happiness at the Expense of Your Co-Workers.* 1st ed. Harper Paperbacks, 1999. Page 174

[55] Bell, Karissa. "Huffington, Sandberg Say Sleep Is Key to Success." Mashable, March 29, 2014. http://mashable.com/2014/03/29/arianna-huffington-sheryl-sandberg/#kTxRX_JZBEqQ.

[56] Crowley, Mark C. "How SAS Became The World's Best Place To Work." *Fast Company,* January 22, 2013. http://www.fastcompany.com/3004953/how-sas-became-worlds-best-place-work.

[57] Delmas, Magali A. and Pekovic, Sanja (2012). "Environmental standards and labor productivity: Understanding the mechanisms that sustain sustainability." Accessed Sept. 26, 2012 via http://onlinelibrary.wiley.com/doi/10.1002/job.1827/pdf

[58] McKeown, Greg. "99% of Networking Is a Waste of Time." *Harvard Business Review,* January 22, 2013. https://hbr.org/2015/01/99-of-networking-is-a-waste-of-time.

[59] INEMURI. (n.d.). Definitions.net. Retrieved May 23, 2016, from http://www.definitions.net/definition/INEMURI.

[60] INEMURI. (n.d.). Definitions.net. Retrieved May 23, 2016, from http://www.definitions.net/definition/INEMURI.

[61] Wilson, Mark. "Meet Ben Barry, Facebook's Minister Of Propaganda." *Fast Company,* CO.Design, November 5, 2012. http://www.fastcodesign.com/1671050/meet-ben-barry-facebooks-minister-of-propaganda.

[62] "Playground Equipment and Play Equipment Solutions from Massey And Harris" http://www.masseyandharris.com/node/153

[63] "History of Patagonia—A Company Created by Yvon Chouinard" http://www.patagonia.com/company-history.html

[64] Brunner, Leslie, Jim Kizielewicz, Jim Gemmell, and Raj Aggarwal. "For Tech Firms, Culture Is King." Interview by Michael Farrel. *Boston Globe.* November 11, 2014. http://archive.boston.com/business/technology/2013/11/17/for-tech-firms-culture-king/C6lxlVEyr4pzqRl5xJe23M/story.html.

[65] Choi, Candice. "'Breastaurants' Experiencing A Mini-Boom." *Huffington Post,* June 24, 2012. http://www.huffingtonpost.com/2012/06/24/breastaurants-mini-boom_n_1622223.html?utm_hp_ref=mostpopular.

[66] https://archive.google.com/mentalplex/